Lotus Elite, Eclat and Excel

An Enthusiast's Guide

Lotus Elite, Eclat and Excel

An Enthusiast's Guide

Matthew Vale

THE CROWOOD PRESS

First published in 2016 by
The Crowood Press Ltd
Ramsbury, Marlborough
Wiltshire SN8 2HR

www.crowood.com

British Library Cataloguing-in-Publication Data
A catalogue record for this book is available from the British Library.

ISBN 978 1 78500 078 2

Acknowledgements
Thanks are due to Mike Kimberley, formally Chief Engineer and CEO of Lotus, and
Mike Taylor of Lotusbits for taking the time to be interviewed and photographed by
me. Also, many thanks to John Walsh, Martin Bradley, Tony Poll and Leigh Greenham
for allowing me to interview them and photograph their cars, and The Oxfordshire
Golf Hotel and Spa for the use of their site for photography of Leigh's Elite. And of
course thanks to my long-suffering wife Julia and daughter Lizzy for putting up with
me disappearing into my study to write this book. Thanks to Group Lotus PLC for
permission to use various images throughout the book.

Lotus press images courtesy of Group Lotus plc.

Nomenclature
In some sources, including some – but not all – published by Lotus, 'Eclat' is rendered
as 'Éclat'. However, as the majority of sources do not use the accent, 'Eclat' without
an accent has been used throughout for the sake of consistency.

Designed and typeset by Guy Croton Publishing Services, Tonbridge, Kent

Printed and bound in India by Replika Press Pvt. Ltd.

CONTENTS

CHAPTER 1   BACKGROUND TO THE LOTUS ELITE   6

CHAPTER 2   DESIGN AND DEVELOPMENT OF THE LOTUS ELITE AND ECLAT   42

CHAPTER 3   THE ECLAT – PRODUCTION AND DEVELOPMENT   96

CHAPTER 4   THE LOTUS TYPE 89 EXCEL (1982–1992)   108

CHAPTER 5   OWNING AND RUNNING   126

Index   143

CHAPTER ONE

BACKGROUND TO THE LOTUS ELITE

INTRODUCTION

The Lotus Type 75 Elite was introduced in May 1974 and was a four-seat GT car aimed at the discerning, well-off, middle-aged driver who needed a car with four full-sized seats to carry one's family or business associates but also wanted the good performance, handling and roadholding that had always marked out Lotus's previous offerings. In a way the new Elite was a logical progression from the Elan Plus 2; another view was that it was a radical first step into the luxury car market for Lotus. Either way, the Elite was a bold move both in car size and market position for Lotus, and Lotus wanted to capitalize on the larger margins that could be made on a car that was a size up from the Elan.

While the Elite retained Lotus's 'trade mark' pop-up headlights, its styling was completely different to previous Lotus models. In the 1970s the latest styling trend was for an aerodynamic wedge shape, along with a lot more straight lines and fewer curves. The Elite adopted these trends to

The Elite was a four-seater, two-door coupé with sports car handling and performance while cosseting its passengers. The car had distinctive styling and took Lotus upmarket. GROUP LOTUS PLC

The Elite was powered by Lotus's own state-of-the-art, 2-litre, twin-cam motor. With twin carbs the engine put out some 160bhp to give the Elite adequate performance.

produce a startlingly up to date appearance, with a low, smooth front blending into the higher cabin area which maintained its line to the back of the car, giving plenty of passenger headroom and a clean two-box shape. The styling was enhanced by the use of a near vertical, clean cut-off at the rear, with the rear window doubling up as a hatch-back – a look first seen in the Reliant Scimitar GTE and which suited the Elite, but this feature did make for a somewhat 'heavy' looking rear quarter. Although it only had two doors, their length and wide opening made access to the heavily sculptured rear seats relatively easy. The Elite had active and passive safety built into the design, with excellent handling and roadholding and an extremely strong passenger cabin.

The Elite was equipped with the then new Lotus 907 engine, a state-of-the-art, 2-litre, 4-cylinder,

16-valve double overhead cam unit. This was coupled to Lotus's own five-speed gearbox which used Austin Maxi internals to give good if not spectacular performance, with a 0–60mph time of 7–8sec and a top speed of 125–128mph (201–206km/h). Fuel consumption was very good for the size and performance of the car at 26–28mpg (10.9–10.1ltr/100km), a result of the car's light weight – its unladen weight was only 2,450lb (1,111kg) – efficient engine and good aerodynamics.

The Elite gave rise to two derivatives, the Eclat and the Excel. The Eclat was a restyled coupé version, sacrificing the Elite's unique rear styling and good rear passenger headroom for a more stylish exterior. With its more conventional coupé styling, the Eclat was more mainstream than the Elite and was in the end a better seller, spawning the Excel, the last of the Elite-inspired family.

THE DON SAFETY TROPHY

First awarded in 1965, the Don Safety Trophy aimed to 'promote the continuing development of vehicle safety standards through good engineering design and innovation; to encourage the use of such new developments and to acclaim those who advance these aims'. The trophy was presented yearly to a vehicle or component manufacturer that met these aims and in 1975 the Lotus Elite was the recipient.

Originally conceived by Don International Ltd, a subsidiary of Manchester-based Small & Parkes (a vehicle component manufacturer that still manufactures commercial vehicle brake components under the TMD Friction Group), the Don Trophy was an important driver of vehicle safety during the 1960s and 1970s. A panel of safety experts considered entries from all car manufacturers, but all the entries had to be in production and being used regularly at the time of submission, so this was a serious attempt to reward actual exponents of safety.

The Elite won the trophy in the year after the car was launched, and joined other worthy winning British cars such as the Range Rover (1970), the Jaguar XJ6 (1968) and the Jensen FF (1965). The award based on the many safety features that were incorporated into the design of the Elite, including the strong passenger cell (the 'ring of steel'); door beams; rollover protection; front and rear impact absorbing bumpers; inertia reel seat belts; and many other features leading to the car exceeding many international safety standards by 100 per cent.

The original press release stated:

Whilst recognizing the limited clientele for the Elite owing to its price and the sporting type of vehicle it represents, the Panel nevertheless felt the successful use of GRP body construction plus the wide margin by which the Elite meets the US and European legal and safety requirements and the emphasis placed on reduction of the risk of fire in the case of a collision, allied to good fuel economy and low emission of pollutants, added up to a substantial improvement, in terms of both primary and secondary safety in a high performance car.

Another telling line from the citation stated that:

Many manufacturers go to great lengths to show the public pictures of cars repeatedly hitting concrete walls. From the conception of the Elite, Lotus concentrated their attention equally to designing the car in such a way that it can avoid hitting walls in the first place and provide the secondary safety structure just in case the wall moves!

The award gives details of the results of the Elite's crash tests in terms of what the standards permit and what the Elite achieved (see table opposite).

The Don Trophy was awarded to the Elite as a result of the attention paid to passive and active safety in the car's design.

Type of test	Required result	Lotus Elite result
1) Steering wheel displacement in 30mph barrier collision	Maximum permissible: 5in (12.7cm)	0.5in (1.27cm)
2) Roof crush resistance when subject to 1.5 times vehicle weight	Maximum allowable deflection of 5in (12.7cm)	3in (7.62cm)
3) Side impact resistance rigidly in place – force needed to deflect door by 6in (15.24cm)	2,250lb (1,020.6kg)	3,400lb (1,542.24kg)
4) Side impact resistance – force needed to deflect door by 12in (30.48cm)	3,500lb (1,587.6kg)	4,700lb (2,131.92kg)
5) Peak force (i.e. door failure)	4,774lb (2,165.48kg)	8,200lb (3,719.52kg)

All in all the figures were pretty impressive and Lotus certainly deserved to win the Don Trophy with the Elite.

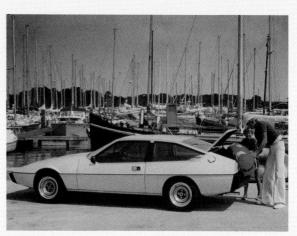

The first evolution of the Elite was the Eclat, which replaced the Elite's rear hatch with a conventional boot and had coupé styling.
GROUP LOTUS PLC

The Elite on the right is partnered by a pair of later Excels.

The Excel, launched in 1983, replaced both the Eclat and the Elite, and was a 2+2 with a lightly restyled Eclat type exterior, retaining the coupé outline and having a significant number of mechanical improvements under the skin, mostly taken from the Toyota parts bin. The Excel remained in production until 1992 and was generally considered to be the car that the Elite and Eclat should have been from the start – a refined and sophisticated car that could compete head-on with the best of the world's competition.

The table on the opposite page gives the timeline of the Elite family of cars, showing the dates of the launch and end of production of the various models in the range.

A Personal Interest

The author must confess to some personal interest in the Elite. When it was released I was impressed with its unique styling and appreciated the performance and economy given by the Lotus engine, and in the late 1980s my father actually bought a silver Series 1 Eclat. When he asked a family friend who was a car nut (Jaguar E-Type and Aston Martin DB2) and eminent engineer for advice he was told 'Don't do it' followed by 'If you must, make sure all the fluids are kept up to the correct level all the time' – sage advice for anyone running a classic. The Eclat was not a success; my father really enjoyed driving it and appreciated the performance and handling but it had reached the age where it had had a couple of careful owners and a lot of careless ones, who had spent nothing on maintaining it and abused it roundly. It really needed a sympathetic owner who had deep pockets; Dad was pretty good about doing what needed to be done to it but recognized that it needed a lot more time and effort spent on it than he was prepared to put in. It didn't help that

Car	Event	Date
Elite	Announcement	June 1974
Elite	First customer delivery	December 1974
Elite	US launch	Late 1974/early 1975
Eclat	Launch announcement	October 1975
Elite 504 (Automatic)	Launch	October 1975
Eclat 504 (Automatic)	Launch and available	Early 1976
US Market Eclat (Sprint)	US launch	Mid-1976
UK Market Eclat Sprint	UK launch	1977
Elite and Eclat S2.2	UK launch	1980
Elite and Eclat Riviera	UK launch	1981
Eclat Excel	UK launch	Oct 1982
Eclat SE	UK launch	Nov 1983
Eclat	End of production	1992

The final member of the Elite family was the Excel. This model was extensively modified mechanically from the original Elite, and took on the Eclat's coupé styling.

LOTUS MODEL NUMBERING

Throughout this book there are references to various Lotus 'Type' numbers – such as the 'Lotus Elite Type 75'. All Lotus cars, be they road or racing models, were assigned a type number, starting retrospectively at 1. The first of the four-seat Elites was Type 75 and the Eclat was Type 76. The following table gives the type numbers of those cars relevant to the Elite story.

Type no.	Model	Production years	Notes
14	Elite (Original)	1957–61	The original Lotus Elite
26	Elan S1 and S2	1962–64	Early open top Elans
36	Elan S3 and S4 FHC	1965–72	Elan Fixed Head Coupé
45	Elan S3 and S4 DHC	1966–72	Last of the baby open Elan
50	Elan Plus 2	1968–74	Predecessor of the Elite
75	Elite	1975–79	Retrospectively both
76	Eclat	1975–79	known as Series 1
83	Elite Series 2.2	1980–82	Badged as Series 2.2 to
84	Eclat Series 2.2	1980–82	reflect increased engine size
89	Excel	1982–92	Last incarnation of the
			four-seater Lotus family

The front end of the Eclat was identical to the Elite. The black grill at the front of the bonnet ducted hot air away from the radiator, which was buried in the nose.

my mother was less than impressed with it as well, so he part-exchanged it for a new 2.0i MG Maestro which actually proved to be a very good car.

Many years later in the early 2010s I bought a bright yellow automatic Elite 504 (from Lotusbits – see Chapter 5) as a project. It was a nice car, which had had a new chassis fitted, but needed a complete suspension overhaul and a good tidy up.

While I completed the suspension work successfully, unfortunately I didn't have the time to get the car fully up together and had the offer of a Lotus Elan Plus 2 project so I had to sell it on. But I still retain a soft spot for the Elite and was severely tempted by offers of various project cars from Mike Taylor of Lotusbits when I visited him to interview him for this book.

LOTUS THE COMPANY

Racing Pedigree

The origins of the Lotus Company date back to the late 1940s when engineer and entrepreneur Colin Anthony Bruce Chapman built a couple of Austin Seven-based trials specials in the stables behind his father's pub in Tottenham, north London. After leaving the RAF in 1949 and joining the civil engineering firm Cousins, followed by a quick move to a better paid job at the British Aluminium Company, Chapman produced a single-seater sports car aimed directly at motor racing built to the 750 Motor Club racing rules. The Lotus Mark III won numerous races in the 1950 season and on the back of such success the Lotus Engineering Company was set up in July 1952, with Chapman and his future wife Hazel Williams as the directors. A range of sports/racing cars were produced by the company through the early 1950s, always made in limited numbers, culminating in the Lotus VI which was much more successful, and was supplied in kit form to avoid tax.

The Lotus VI is considered by some to be the first 'real' Lotus as it was the first of Chapman's cars to have a Lotus-designed chassis, rather than the modified Austin Seven chassis used in the previous cars. Even at this early stage in his career, Chapman had demonstrated the important traits that would influence all of his future designs:

• add lightness
• make things do more than one job if possible
• interpret the rule book to your advantage.

Early examples of 'adding lightness' included the use of aluminium for all bodywork – which as well as being light was easily worked, widely available and relatively cheap – and the Mark VI's light and strong tubular chassis. Making things do two or more jobs was demonstrated by the use of the tubular body frame to brace the Austin Seven chassis of his first Mark III. Chapman's elegant interpretation of the rule books included the clever modification of the standard Austin Seven engine's two-port head into a four-port head to give a significant power boost in the Lotus Mark III, and the selling of cars in kit form to enable his customers to legally avoid paying car tax.

The first serious 'production' Lotus was the VI. This was a simple car with proprietary mechanicals but using a Lotus-designed, tubular space-frame chassis and alloy bodywork.

MIKE KIMBERLEY – FATHER OF THE LOTUS ELITE

Born in 1938, Michael John Kimberley C. Eng, F.I. Mech. E., FRSA, FIED, F.I.M.I. was the chief engineer at Lotus when the Elite was being developed and played a pivotal role in its design, production and ongoing development. A dyed-in-the-wool engineer who worked in the motor industry for all his life, Mike started his career as an apprentice at Jaguar in 1954 and by 1965 he was working for the company's legendary engineer Bill Heynes and designer Malcolm Sayer. He led the special projects team that designed and developed the XJ13, Jaguar's then secret Le Mans racer project powered by a quad-cam, 5.5-litre V12. He also ran the project that resulted in the introduction of the V12-powered E-Type Series III in 1971. While he was at Jaguar he developed a specialization in vehicle engineering and dynamics and this stood him in good stead when he joined Lotus in 1969 as manager of continuous engineering.

Mike's early responsibilities at Lotus included such fire-fighting tasks as improving the reliability of the Elan and the Elan Plus 2 and becoming project leader and designer of the Lotus Europa Twin Cam. By 1972 he was Lotus's chief engineer, heading a team of three that would be responsible for the design and development of the Lotus Elite, Eclat/Excel and the initiation of the Esprit. Mike's fellow team members were Tony Rudd, Lotus's technical director, who had responsibility for the engine, and Oliver ('Olly') Winterbottom, who was the stylist/designer. The team worked closely with Colin Chapman, chairman of Lotus, to produce a car that was light, fast, reliable, efficient and economical while retaining the Lotus core values of excellent performance, handling and roadholding – and hence good primary safety – and meeting all current and expected global safety and emissions legislation.

When interviewed for this book, Mike was particularly proud of the Elite's advanced design and extensive safety features, and the way the team managed to meet Chapman's often

Mike Kimberley, pictured here with his presentation copy of the Don Safety Trophy, was responsible for much of the design and development of the Elite family of Lotuses.

very demanding requirements in a car that remained in production for close to twenty years with minimal changes to any of the design fundamentals. The car won the Don Safety Trophy after its launch, which validated all the effort that the team put into its design, and was heralded in the press as 'tomorrow's car today' in recognition of its many ground-breaking design features. For example, in the 30mph barrier crash test, steering wheel displacement used only ½in of the 5in allowed in the regulations.

From an engineering perspective Mike emphasized how the design had to be simple and elegant, resulting in a design in which individual elements of the car often did two or more jobs.

continued overleaf

Mike Kimberley – Father of the Lotus Elite *continued*

Mike Kimberley (right), Colin Chapman (centre) and Olly Winterbottom pictured at Mike's drawing board in the Lotus factory. With Tony Rudd, this was the team who managed the design and production of the Elite. GROUP LOTUS PLC

The car was designed by a small, tightly knit team with strong leadership which resulted in an outstanding product that went into production after only a couple of years of development. As well as this, Chapman was very 'hands-on' in the design process and had a major influence on the design of the car. The rear suspension was a case in point, with Chapman insisting on the driveshafts being used as the upper suspension link, overruling Mike's suggestion of a separate upper link and unstressed driveshafts. (Mike did get his own back by sneaking a touch of Ackermann geometry into the front suspension to enhance the steering feel while Chapman was opposed to any being dialled into the geometry.) However, much of Chapman's influence on the team and the application of a very thoughtful design process can be seen by the large number of elegant and simple design features, usually making a part do more than one job. Mike was especially pleased with the special bolts used to lock the highly stressed front anti-roll bar (also front suspension shunt/wheel location member) to the car, which also doubled up to mount the front of the chassis to the bodyshell.

Another example of clever and innovative design was the side impact intrusion protection. The body's door striker plate was bolted to a plate that was in turn welded to the tubular anti-roll bar in the B-pillar. The welds on the plate were designed to 'peel' if there was a side impact, limiting the deformation of the welded plate and the intrusion of the door and its internal steel beam in a controlled manner. This resulted in a superb level of resistance to side impacts.

Another neat solution addressed the need for quick fuel-tank filling and absolute safety in a rear impact or if the car was rolled over; which was the design of the fuel tank, the fuel fillers and the tank's mounting in the car. The twin fuel filler pipes were connected flexibly through large-bore pipes to the tank, enabling the tank to be filled quickly without air locks. The pipes were designed to prevent fuel spillage if the car was turned on its side or upside down, in anticipation of future US safety standards. By mounting it in the centre of the car between the rear crash beams and the spare wheel, the fuel tank was protected from rear impacts and would survive test impacts with no damage.

Testing the Elite

During the car's design process, once the first prototypes were up and running, part of the development process required Mike and Tony and others to undertake long-distance proving runs across Europe to thoroughly test the car. Every couple of weeks Mike and Tony would hop into the test car on a Friday afternoon, drive down to Dover and take the hovercraft across to Calais. They would then drive across France, through Switzerland, taking the Alpine passes, and down into Italy and onto the Autostrada del Sole (the Motorway of the Sun – which sounds a lot better than the British M1) for the fast journey south to Rome. Then it was once around the Coliseum (awful traffic) and off out of Rome along the old Mille Miglia (Thousand Miles) endurance race route to Brescia in northern Italy, then head west out

The front view of the Elite shows the pronounced 'wedge' shape – the styling feature of the 1970s that was adopted by most manufacturers. Pop-up headlights aided aerodynamics and enhanced the lines. GROUP LOTUS PLC

of Italy into the South of France and a dinner stop and the only night's sleep in Monte Carlo. From there it was a blast up the French autoroutes, round Paris's Boulevard Périphérique (again it sounds better than the English prosaic 'Ring Road') and back to Calais and Dover to arrive at Hethel on Monday morning having covered 2,973 miles (Mike remembers the mileage exactly). Any faults and issues with the car would be identified and fixed and then tested in the next long-distance run.

Mike recalls two incidents while carrying out this regime – one that could have been very serious, and one that illustrates the type of problem that could be identified. The first incident happened early on in the testing regime while in the Alps. Mike was driving and Tony was dozing in the passenger seat (they shared the driving and sleeping to get the miles in) when Mike approached a tight right-hand bend. He

was pressing on, Chapman style, and in those days the outer edge of the road was marked only with white painted bollards. With a drop of over 7,000ft (2,000m) to his left and no crash barrier, Mike wound on the steering lock, on a gravelly edge, only to find that it was not enough and he was not going to make it round the bend. Luckily the brakes worked – a testament to the suspension and balance of the car – and the car ended up with its left-hand wheel just on the edge; and a by then fully awake and very agitated Tony in the passenger seat with a spectacular (possibly too spectacular for comfort) view from the passenger window. It was a lucky escape for the pair of them and the steering rack and geometry was swiftly revised when they returned to Hethel and the problem was solved.

continued overleaf

Mike Kimberley – Father of the Lotus Elite *continued*

The second – less dramatic – event was when they had a puncture on a steeply inclined road down to a Swiss village. Mike was told by Tony to change the wheel as Tony outranked Mike as he was the technical director. Mike describes how Tony 'sat on a wall waving his legs and joking' while Mike set to and found out how useless the wheel jack was – another item that was changed after their return to Hethel.

Doing It Chapman's Way

Working closely with Colin Chapman gave Mike an insight into the man. He found Chapman a fair and charismatic boss – he said that people would follow him off the edge of a cliff – and contrary to some portrayals he found Chapman to be a hard but fair and reasonable boss – but a boss who knew his own mind and what he wanted. Mike would often have 'debates' with Chapman (for example, about the Elite's rear suspension, as described above), but he found that Chapman respected people who could argue with him as long as the argument was based on solid knowledge – Chapman had little time for people who couldn't back up their arguments with facts, and even less time for yes-men.

Mike recalled a typical example of Chapman's fair and generous behaviour. After a long argument about one particular design, Chapman asked Mike who the chairman was. Mike replied that Chapman was and Chapman said, 'Well do it this [his] way' – so Mike did. Three months later there was a need for some rapid remedial action due to the chairman's decision, and Mike implemented his solution. After the problem was solved, Chapman came up to Mike in the open-plan office at Hethel, shook his hand, thanked him publicly for being right and for sorting out the problem, and presented him with 500 Group Lotus shares.

Rising through the Lotus Ranks

Mike was appointed managing director of Lotus Cars in 1976. After Chapman's untimely death from a heart attack in 1982, Mike was appointed to the Group Lotus plc board and CEO in 1984. Mike was pivotal in negotiating Toyota's help and investment in the company in early 1983 which enabled Lotus to survive after Chapman's death. He also used the Toyota parts bin to re-engineer the Eclat to produce the much improved and cheaper to produce Excel, which included the redesigned rear suspension that didn't use the driveshafts as load-bearing items – Mike eventually got his own way on that issue.

Mike continued to work at Lotus and took the company through the 1980s and into the 1990s. Part of his strategy to save and grow Lotus was to promote Lotus Engineering, the engineering technology and consultancy side of the business, as a vital symbiotic adjunct to car production and sales globally. As head of the operational executives, he took Lotus from 9p per share in December 1982 to 129.5p per share in January 1986 at the eventual takeover of Lotus by GM. This also resulted in a period of financial stability.

Mike left Lotus in January 1992 to become executive vice president of General Motors Overseas Corporation in South East Asia. After working for a number of other automotive companies, including Lamborghini in Italy and TATA in India, Mike successfully returned to Lotus as CEO of Group Lotus in May 2006, where he initiated the Evora and V6 Exige. He eventually retired in 2009 at the age of seventy-one.

The original **Elite** was a two-seater coupé, with a glass-fibre monocoque and a Coventry Climax engine.
Produced from the late 1950s through to the early 1960s, it was more of a racer than a GT car.

Production of the Lotus VI continued through the 1950s, and with production approaching 100 gave Lotus some financial stability. Post 1955 the VI was replaced with the sports racing VIII, IX, X and 11 (note that Lotus changed to Arabic numbering with the '11'), and the pure racer Mark 12, which was designed to compete in Formula 1 and 2.

Lotus's First Road Cars

The Type 14 Elite marked Lotus's first foray into the world of road cars. Announced at the 1957 Earls Court Motor Show alongside a more production-friendly replacement for the Mk VI in the shape of the Lotus Seven, the Lotus Elite was a GT car, with the virtually unique concept of a monocoque made entirely out of glass fibre with bonded-in steel reinforcement for high stress areas such as suspension pick-up points and engine mounts. The Elite had two design aims: to win its class in the Le Mans 24 Hours race and to be an excellent two-seater GT road car.

The original Elite turned out to be a bit too much of a racer, winning its class at Le Mans several years running but proving to be a bit less refined on the road than a true GT car should be. In addition, its glass-fibre monocoque proved to be expensive to make and its bespoke Coventry Climax FWE engine was expensive to buy resulting in the car's price being high. Its replacement in the road-car market, the 1962 Lotus Elan, was the road car that the Elite should have been. With its rust-free, glass-fibre body and simple but stiff steel backbone chassis, it positioned Lotus exactly where it needed to be – with a cutting edge, sophisticated, civilized, fast, fine-handling road car that was simple and economical to make and met the pent-up demand for just such a vehicle.

The Lotus Elan was a small, relatively cheap two-seat sports car with a Lotus twin-cam engine. Its handling, roadholding and ride set a standard that other manufacturers still struggle to meet today.

The Lotus Europa was a small mid-engine sports car produced between 1966 and 1975. Originally Renault-powered, it later used the Ford-based Lotus Twin Cam engine.

The Lotus Plus 2 was the first Lotus four-seater, although the rear seats were for children only. It was the precursor of the Elite.

The Elan was powered by Lotus's first engine, the Lotus Twin Cam, with its alloy twin-camshaft head and timing cover mated to the Ford 116E bottom end. This engine gave Lotus a powerful state-of-the-art unit that was relatively cheap to produce and ensured the Elan's success. This enabled Lotus to finance their ever more ambitious racing programme and also made it possible for the company to buy new premises based on an old Second World War aerodrome in Hethel, Norfolk. As well as being somewhere for Chapman to keep his aeroplane, Hethel was big enough to accommodate the increase in production needed to meet demand and had a ready-made test track around the aerodrome's perimeter.

Lotus followed up the Elan with the mid-engined Europa, using a Renault engine and transmission. This appeared in 1966 and the Elan Plus 2, a larger version of the original Elan, followed in 1967. The Plus 2 gave Lotus a foothold in the upmarket 2+2

coupé market and was the first Lotus – in 1969 in Plus 2S form – to be supplied only in fully assembled form from the factory.

As the 1960s turned into the 1970s, Lotus was looking to move upmarket, and design of the new 900 series engine and a car to put it in had commenced. Production of the two-seat Elan was finished in August 1973, while the Plus 2 continued in production until December 1974, and the Europa was eventually phased out in March 1975. Lotus put the new Model 50 Elite into production during 1974, with the first deliveries being made towards the end of the year. As the 1970s progressed, Lotus the company was performing reasonably well, with the Elite and Eclat (along with the mid-engined Esprit which was introduced in 1975) selling well and with external engineering consultancy work, including the engineering of the DeLorean DMC-12 sports car, adding to the company's revenue and building a strong reputation in the motor industry.

The DeLorean was one of the projects that Lotus worked on in the 1970s. Lotus provided engineering consultancy to get the car into production.

The Toyota and GM Years

By 1980 Lotus had identified that it needed to produce a smaller car to increase the numbers of cars it produced and recognized that it needed a partner to assist it. Mike Kimberley approached Toyota in the early 1980s and struck a deal whereby Lotus would carry out engine development and engineering consultancy work for them in return for preferential access to Toyota components in order to assist Lotus in updating the ageing mechanicals of the Elite and Eclat and to source the drivetrain for a projected new small sports car that would reintroduce the Elan. The deal resulted in the provision of a Toyota gearbox and final drive in the Excel along with various other parts including the brakes, and the deal was extended in 1983 with Toyota buying a 22.5 per cent share of equity in the company. However, in 1982, Chapman, the leading light of the company, died of a heart attack while at the same time the company came under investigation for fraud related to the DeLorean project and revenue from car sales plummeted due to the oil crisis killing sales of new cars. Lotus managed to weather this storm, mainly through its engineering consultancy business, but by December 1985 Lotus were in a bit of a fix, with two of the company's major shareholders feeling they were unable to continue investing in the company.

Lotus management recognized that Lotus needed a single, large company to own it and provide the ongoing investment needed to develop new cars. The saviour of the company was GM who bought a controlling stake in Lotus on 14 January 1985, and followed this up later by acquiring all the equity in the company, buying out Toyota in the process. The Excel continued in production alongside the Esprit but much effort was being put into getting a new GM-based Elan replacement – the M100 Elan – designed and into production. The Excel continued to be produced alongside the Esprit and the Elan M100, eventually ceasing production in 1992 when GM finally pulled the plug on Lotus and sold the company to the Bugatti company owned by Italian Romano Artioli.

LOTUS ELITE PRODUCTION HISTORY

Moving Upmarket

The Lotus Elite – Lotus Type 75 and sometimes called the M50 Elite because of its Lotus project number of 'M50' – was placed into production in 1973 and attracted a great deal of attention from the press of the day. Lotus was nearly unique at the time as it was a manufacturer of road cars, but also

**The Elite was a striking car, especially from the rear, where its
all-glass rear hatch dominates the lines.**

had a thriving racing car side which competed in the top international racing formulas; probably only Ferrari could boast such a wide product range. This was no surprise as the company's founder, Colin Chapman, was a keen competitor and in the early days of the company sold cars to effectively finance his racing. As the company moved into the 1970s, Chapman was keen to move it upmarket and the Elite was seen as the means of doing just that.

As a full four-seater, the Elite was seen as a step up from the Elan Plus 2. Chapman was an intelligent and talented engineer and entrepreneur and he knew that the margins on producing a small car, such as the Elan, were considerably smaller than those generated by a bigger car that could be sold at a significantly higher price. While Lotus had been a member of the SMMT (Society of Motor Manufacturers and Traders) since 1955 and had been building complete cars for customers for some years Chapman still felt the need to cast off Lotus's reputation as a kit-car manufacturer and join the ranks of the 'real' car

makers – as well as making a profit to finance the racing car side of Lotus, which was his first love. The mature, upmarket and practical Elite would fulfil those ambitions, all the more so as it was powered by Lotus's first complete engine, the double overhead camshaft, 16-valve '907' unit. Finally, the Elite reflected Chapman's changing tastes as he grew older. He was born in 1928, and he designed and produced stripped-out, racing-oriented cars, including the original Elite and culminating in the Seven, during the 1950s while he was in his twenties. The next milestone came in the 1960s when, while in his thirties and still designing his pure racing cars, Chapman designed the relatively civilized, but sporting, two-seater Elan road car. As Chapman turned forty in 1968, family commitments and maturing tastes gave rise to the larger and relatively luxurious Elan Plus 2 which could seat two adults and two children. The Plus 2 was a lot more refined than the Elan, and as it aged it gained more fixtures and fittings to become a junior luxury GT car. Importantly, as

This brochure shot of the Elite emphasizes the low build and style of the car. GROUP LOTUS PLC

a first step away from the kit-car image, when the first update to the Plus 2, the Plus 2S, was launched in 1969, it was only available as a factory-built car. When he reached his mid-forties, Chapman produced the 'new' Elite – a 'grown-up' grand tourer that could seat four adults in comfort and was aimed at long continental trips down to Cannes or Monaco or as a respectable sports car in which to take clients out for lunch rather than for hooning around the country lanes.

To summarise, there were three compelling reasons for Lotus to produce a car like the Elite: the elevation of Lotus to a 'serious' manufacturer;

the prospect of higher margins and hence profit; and the gradual ageing of Lotus's core market of drivers who liked sports cars but had need of a more practical family car that was comfortable and civilized but could still perform and handle to sports-car standards.

Making the Elite Future-Proof

The design team responsible for the Elite was based at the Lotus factory at Hethel in Norfolk, England, and comprised Mike Kimberley (product engineering manager), Oliver Winterbottom (designer) and Tony Rudd (chief engineer) along with Chapman.

The Lotus factory at Hethel in Norfolk was a new building on a Second World War airfield. The airfield provided a landing strip for Chapman's light aircraft and the perimeter track provided a ready-made test track. GROUP LOTUS PLC

The Lotus engine had twin overhead camshafts, 4 valves per cylinder and the bores were slanted at 45 degrees to give the unit a low profile.

Design of the M50 Elite project started in earnest in March 1971 and by January 1972 a running car existed. One of the many design imperatives that the Elite was intended to meet was being future-proof. Chapman was increasingly frustrated by the effort needed to keep the Elan and Europa compliant with the ever-increasing raft of emissions and safety legislation that Lotus needed to meet in order to sell into various important markets, including the United States, Europe and the UK. Each new regulation meant diverting engineering effort into meeting them, which Chapman saw as wasted effort, especially as any change would need to be tested and approved by the relevant national body. As well as taking up precious engineering resources, the changes often led to cars made for different markets differing significantly from each other and causing problems on the production lines and in stock holdings. So when the Elite was being designed the engineering team looked at all present and proposed future legislation in Lotus's major markets and the car was designed to meet or exceed the most stringent. This approach had a number of advantages: it cut down the need for 'bolt-on' fixes as standards changed; it meant there were very few market-specific parts required; and it meant that Lotus could legitimately claim that the car met or exceeded all existing safety legislation, a claim that helped it win the prestigious Don Safety Trophy in 1975.

Engine-wise the 907 motor was also designed to be as efficient as possible, and this meant it was also relatively clean in terms of emissions. In fact, when it was introduced to the US market, the Elite did not need any of the bolt-on, power-sapping, emission-control mechanisms such as air pumps and catalysts used by other manufacturers to meet US requirements. These emissions were progressively tightened up and the 907 did eventually have to have some emissions-specific equipment added, but the impact on the engine's performance was a lot less than that experienced by other manufacturers.

Launch of the Elite

While the Elite was launched just in time for the first of the 1970s' fuel crises, which hit the sales of cars generally, the Elite was in fact quite well placed to catch sales from the larger-engined, gas-guzzling competition as its relatively efficient engine, light weight and good aerodynamics gave it relatively good fuel consumption. The Elite, with its high-tech mechanicals, luxury interior and up-to-the-minute looks, was greeted by the world's press with a mixture of respect and astonishment. Respect as it was an excellent product that showed the world that Lotus had really broken into the big time with the car, and astonishment that the car had preserved the Lotus DNA in terms of performance, handling and roadholding while providing a practical and stylish full four-seater.

The Elite sold in reasonable numbers and justified Lotus's move to the new market niche. Although sales in 1973 were only 6 due to difficulties in getting the car into production, 1974 saw a total of 687 being manufactured as production ramped up to meet the pent-up demand. The Elite was marketed in various specifications – from 501 to 504 – with the 504 version, boasting a Borg Warner BW35 three-speed automatic gearbox, being introduced at the Earls Court Motor Show in October 1975.

Development of the Elite

Eclat

The first development of the Elite was the Type 76 Eclat, launched on 15 October 1975, which retained the Elite's chassis and wheelbase but had a modified 'fastback' rear end giving coupé styling with a conventional boot and slightly decreased headroom for the rear passengers. Intended to be cheaper than the Elite, with a lower specification, the revised body resulted in a weight reduction of approximately 200lb (90kg) and gave slightly better performance than the heavier Elite.

The car's interior was uprated when the Excel was introduced. This picture of a late Excel shows the revised instrument layout.

Leigh Greenham's Elite Series 2 basks in the sunshine outside the Oxfordshire Golf Hotel and Spa.

The model was, like the Elite, marketed in several specifications, with the base model 520 boasting a low spec including narrow 13in steel wheels and four-speed gearbox, while the 521, 522 and 523 boasted various specification tweaks, with all three having Elite-style alloy wheels and five-speed gearbox. The 524 had the same BW35 automatic gearbox as seen in the 504 Elite and was introduced in 1976. The base model Eclat was renamed 'Sprint' for the US market. While some of the 520s sported US market-only alloy wheels the rest of the specification remained the same as for the UK car, with a four-speed gearbox and steel wheels.

Series 2.2

Production of the Elite and Eclat proceeded through the 1970s with only minor changes being made to both models – much of Lotus's engineering resources being devoted to the range-topping, mid-engined Esprit. In 1980 the second versions of the Elite and Eclat were introduced, badged 'Series 2.2' to reflect the use of the enlarged 2174cc Lotus engine. While the body shape was hardly changed, there were a significant number of improvements made in the light of the previous five years of production. The Lotus five-speed gearbox was dropped for a German Getrag unit,

PRODUCTION FIGURES

The following table presents data obtained from a number of sources, including Roy Bacon's book *The Third Generation Lotuses*; information from the Lotus Forums; and the *Book of Automobile Production and Sales Figures 1945–2005* produced by Productioncars.com. The sources all show some variation, and the figures presented below give averages of any variations identified. While the figures are probably not exact, they are certainly not wildly out and give a good indication of the sales trends of the Lotus Elite family.

YEAR	Elite	Eclat	Elite S2.2	Eclat S2.2	Excel	Total
1973	6					6
1974	687					687
1975	459	20				479
1976	451	341				792
1977	210	280				490
1978	293	354				647
1979	276	281				557
1980	20	20	105	101		246
1981			13	31		44
1982			14	91	71	176
1983			1		214	215
1984					315	315
1985					362	362
1986					249	249
1987					336	336
1988					244	244
1989					183	183
1990					113	113
1991					56	56
1992					15	15
Total	2,402	1,296	133	223	2,158	6,212

The last Excels have flared wheel arches and new chin spoilers and sill mouldings, but are still recognizably derived from the original Elite.

although the automatic option retained the Borg Warner box. A zinc-coated chassis addressed longevity issues of the original painted chassis and revised front and rear bumpers (restyled at the rear) enabled the cars to meet the latest impact-resistance legislation. New alloy wheels, some subtle bodywork additions and the repositioning of the Elite's rear wiper to the top of the hatch finished off the external changes.

Excel

The Excel was introduced in 1982, and to retain continuity with the previous models was initially called the Eclat Excel. While retaining the Lotus 2.2 engine and the Eclat's 2+2 body, the Excel featured many subtle revisions to the body style to give a more rounded and contemporary appearance. The Excel came with a new gearbox, differential and rear suspension, mostly Toyota derived, and was generally considered to be a significantly better engineered car than the Elite and the Eclat. The Excel directly replaced the Eclat, and with the Elite being dropped from the range in 1983 it became the only four-seater left in Lotus's range alongside the mid-engined Esprit. The Excel remained in production until 1992, finishing off the eighteen-year production run of the four-seater Lotus models. Lotus's financial situation at the time precluded the replacement of the car.

LEIGH GREENHAM'S 1980 ELITE SERIES 2.2

Leigh Greenham has owned his immaculate 1980 Series 2.2 Elite since 1997. In that time has toured Europe, raced it round tracks and exhibited it at the classic car shows.

Leigh first became aware of the Elite in the early 1980s, when he drew up in his somewhat rusty Lancia HPE alongside a very smart, low, dark blue and brand new Lotus Elite. He was impressed with the looks and the fact that it was carrying four adults and wondered if he could ever afford such a stunning car – the price at the time was around £20,000. In the mid-1990s, Leigh and his wife Kaz decided they wanted a classic car to use as a weekend classic car and after extensive research decided on a Series 2.2 Elite. The main issues of the Series 1 cars – the

gearbox, chassis rust and the weak vacuum-operated headlights – had been fixed on the Series 2.2 with its German-made Getrag gearbox, fully galvanized chassis and electrically lifted headlights. Along with the larger and torquier 2.2 litre engine, the redesigned spoilers and sill extensions, revised rear wash wipe and uprated interior it meant the Series 2.2 car was a much more practical and reliable car.

Leigh took over eighteen months to find the right car; he looked at about twelve but the only two that were in a good enough condition to buy were automatics and Leigh wanted a manual. Finally the car he bought emerged when a Dutch collector, Eugene Van Herpen, decided to sell off his collection of twelve cars, which included

Leigh Greenham's Elite is in Lotus Essex colours and was driven by Colin Chapman all over Europe back in 1980.

**The distinctive Essex Blue is a Mercedes colour, and Leigh went to the original
Essex stripe manufacturers to get the red cheat lines reproduced.**

a dark blue manual Elite, with air conditioning, power steering and a connection with Colin Chapman. It was exactly what Leigh was looking for.

Leigh arranged with Eugene to visit him to view the car, which was stored in a barn and had not run for a couple of years. Once there, they found the car was covered in dust, the bodyshell had a number of cracks, the windscreen was cracked and the red leather interior was dry and cracked. Worse, the car wouldn't start as the Lumenition was duff. However, it was the best car that Leigh had seen and was the specification he wanted. The clincher was that owner's handbook had Colin Chapman's name on it and Eugene had a letter from Andrew Ferguson at Team Lotus confirming it had been owned by the team in 1980 and 1981. The car had been produced during the Essex Petroleum sponsoring period for Lotus, but although there were always Essex Esprit Turbos around, Colin preferred to use a four-seater. Consequently, this very early Type 83 Elite had been painted Essex Blue, had the same red Connolly leather as the Turbo Esprit and had a thin Essex stripe of red and chrome along its sills (nothing like as brash as the stickers on the Essex Turbo Esprit!). So with the proviso that Eugene got it running and to Amsterdam he bought it for £4,250.

A couple of weeks later, with a new Lumenition fitted and the car in Amsterdam, Leigh took a one-way flight to Schiphol airport where Eugene picked him up in the now roadworthy and running Elite. Leigh drove the car home to Oxfordshire (to quote him, 'with a big smile on my face') via the Hook of Holland ferry, and it performed pretty well, with just a bit of lumpy running below 3,000rpm. Once home he had the car looked

continued overleaf

Leigh Greenham's 1980 Elite Series 2.2 *continued*

**The Elite boot is reasonably roomy. Rumour has it that it was
designed to accommodate a golf bag.**

over by Peter Day. Most of the rubber bushes, mountings and belts were replaced, the brakes were overhauled, and new exhaust valves, windscreen and clutch were fitted. Once that was done the car was given a fresh MOT and Leigh managed to get the DVLA to reissue it with its original UK registration number, LCL 825V.

Next he wanted to fix the cracks in the body and sort out the paint so at the end of 1998 Leigh put it into Robin Alabaster at Aldermaston, who has an excellent reputation for his fibreglass skills, hoping to complete the work in time for the following summer. Leigh had partially dismantled the car before taking it to Robin's workshop, but ensuring that he had the original paint colour

took a bit of research as the L44 paint code on the car's data-plate and original paperwork did not seem to exist. Several other numbers existed for Essex Blue over the years, but he was keen to use the original shade. Fortunately, one of Robin's paint suppliers found a list that cross-referenced L44 to the old Mercedes colour 'Magnetic Blue', and a sample proved it to be the exact shade of metallic paint.

Robin laboriously took the body back to raw fibreglass, filling a mobile phone aerial hole in the roof and fitting a new radiator mounting panel. With the car in bits, Leigh also took the opportunity to recondition the leaky power-steering rack and refurbish the original Speedline

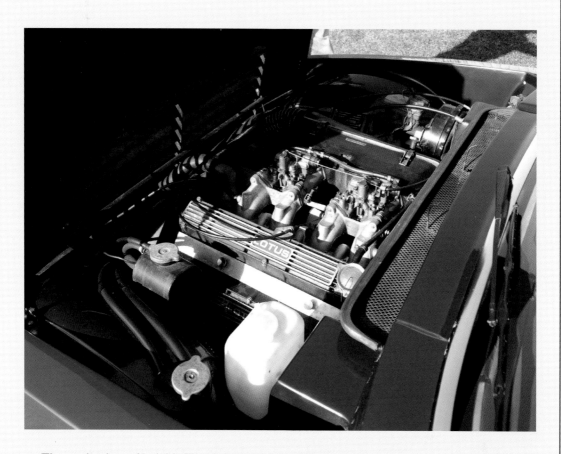

The engine bay of Leigh's Elite is immaculate. The metal strip over the spark plugs was often seen on the original Lotus twin-cam engine to help with electric suppression. A previous owner had put it on Leigh's car.

alloy wheels. The body was primed and painted by the summer of 1999, but due to a house move, Leigh asked Robin to slow the project down so that he could hang on to the car into the autumn until his garage was clear of packing crates.

With Leigh's garage finally cleared early in 2000, Robin and Leigh finished off the remaining tasks on the body of the car. Team Lotus were able to provide the name of the Norfolk company that had made all of the Essex decals and labels and they were still in business and able to produce precisely original stripes for him. The finished bodywork looked fabulous! In fact, it was so good that the faded and cracked leather

interior really had to be attended to, as it was now letting the car down.

The original leather had been supplied by Connolly, whose records showed the exact shade of red that had been used. Mr Tim Connolly actually remembered the car as it was a rush job and they didn't want to let Colin Chapman down. Leigh took the car down to their works in Wimbledon where their expert recommended that the front seat 'horseshoe and bolster' panels needed to be replaced, but the rest of the leather could all be re-coloured back to its original condition.

continued overleaf

Leigh Greenham's 1980 Elite Series 2.2 *continued*

Leigh's Elite is an immaculate example of a unique car. He uses it for continental touring, attending car days and for fun at weekends – roles it fulfils admirably.

They no longer did restoration work themselves but recommended their former subcontractor, Benchmark Renovations in Battersea, who did a marvellous job in just three days.

Let me give you Leigh's opinion of his car, and the trips he has made in it, in his own words:

I am now very pleased with the overall condition of the car, which has been widely admired by both experts and non-experts alike. It drives extremely well, although with over 120,000 miles on the clock, has started to burn a bit of oil, not enough to stop it romping through the MOT emissions test each year. Super-unleaded fuel seems to agree with it (especially Shell V-Power), which is handy when driving the car around the UK and Europe. The Elite was never intended to be an out-and-out performance sports car but more of a long-distance grand tourer, but it is never disgraced on a circuit thanks

to its 0–60mph time of 7.5 seconds and top speed of 130mph. Interestingly, it was originally marketed as a businessman's car, with the radio-cassette unit having a removable microphone, conjuring up an image of the driver dictating memos and letters on his drive into work, then tossing the tape to his secretary as he gets to his office.

During my ownership of the Elite, it has been fun discovering more of its early history while owned by Team Lotus. DVLC offer a service where for a small charge they will supply the owner with photo-

copies of all archived data related to his vehicle. This produced the original licence application handwritten by Lotus in April 1980, as well as the ownership trans-fers and paperwork related to its export to Holland in 1987. The Lotus factory archives were able to give me a copy of the original build specification of the car, including enough detail to show that the key numbers were still the same. At the 1999 Donington festival I bought a copy of the Team Essex Lotus 1981 brochure

continued overleaf

Leigh Greenham's 1980 Elite Series 2.2 *continued*

Series 2.2 badges
and the distinctive
Essex stripe
show this car is
something special.

which contained a review of the 1980 F1 season including a photo of the team buses on the harbour-side at Monaco with my Elite in the foreground! This brochure credited LAT Motorsport for the photos, so a visit to their archive in Twickenham yielded another Monaco picture with the back of the car in full view parked next to an Essex Mini, as well as a picture of Mario Andretti relaxing outside the Team Lotus motorhome at the Spanish Grand Prix with the car in the background.

Another great discovery came via Clive Chapman at Classic Team Lotus. His initial reply to my letter was that there were no records of my car, but some months later when clearing out some old drawers he came across the original insurance file. This contained the original memo from Team Lotus to Lotus Cars formally requesting that an Essex Elite be built for ACBC, insurance cover notes in all of the relevant European languages and ferry tickets for the 1980 Belgian Grand Prix. There was a handwritten

note on Team Lotus headed paper requesting that the service department take special care with LCL 852V as it was Colin Chapman's car, and a two-page letter from the Team's retained driver, Ernie Huppert, concerning an incident that happened when he was transferring the Elite from the Monaco Grand Prix to the Italian GP. In San Remo he misjudged the width of the Elite, and its wing mirror scraped the wing of a parked VW Golf, so he was concerned that maybe an insurance claim. Team Lotus Manager, Andrew Ferguson, wrote to their insurance brokers about it, but nothing more was heard.

As part of my ongoing search into the car's Team Lotus history, in 2003 I contacted Sutton Motorsport's photo archive in Towcester, as I had heard that they had acquired the photos of David Phipps, the Team Lotus photographer from that period. This contact turned out to be fabulous, as they were able to unearth a sequence of photos from the German Grand Prix at Hockenheim in August 1980 where my

A classy car in a classy setting. Leigh's S2.2 Elite outside the Oxfordshire Golf Hotel and Spa.

car had pride of place in the paddock. One particularly posed shot has Colin Chapman, Mario Andretti, Elio de Angelis and a sponsor all grouped around the bonnet. Other photos of the car were taken alongside the Orient Express, which was chartered by Tissot, another Lotus sponsor at the time, and brought to Hockenheim with one hundred or so invited guests aboard. Colin drove the Elite to the sidings for a promotional dinner on the train and was photographed standing in front of the car with two sponsors in fancy dress.

The Essex Petroleum sponsorship deal fell apart midway through 1981, when the Monaco-based company went belly-up and its owner, David Thieme, apparently did time for fraud! Team Lotus sold my Elite through the Lotus dealer Cooper City in London to a Graham T. R. Moody in October 1981, who ran it for six years before selling it to Eugene. I was able to track Graham down and he kindly sent me pictures of the car, which he

had re-registered as ESX 2, outside his home in Twickenham and his holiday home in Spain.

Since I have owned it, the car has enjoyed meeting up with two of its old racing car colleagues from the days of the Formula 1 team. The Type 81B was Nigel Mansell's first Grand Prix car in 1980, still resplendent in its original livery and being raced in the FIA Thoroughbred Grand Prix series at various circuits throughout Europe. Getting pictures of the two cars side-by-side in the paddock at Donington was great fun. Also, the Type 88 has now been restored by Classic Team Lotus; this was also an Essex liveried car, famous for being banned for its innovative twin-chassis in 1981, and has more recently been shown at the Goodwood Festival of Speed and raced in the TGP series.

continued overleaf

Leigh Greenham's 1980 Elite Series 2.2 *continued*

Rewards

So, where have we taken the Elite over the years since its restoration? Summer 2000 saw us on the Portsmouth to Cherbourg ferry for a holiday in Normandy, and we also did one of our first club events, the Lotus Drivers Club trip to Hethel for a factory tour and trip to the Team Lotus warehouse in Wymondham. In 2001 I was pleased to get the car onto the Castle Combe circuit for the first time for a few high-speed laps alongside other Lotus cars, old and new. In 2002, a similar thrill was experienced at Zandvoort at the Club Lotus Holland 25th anniversary event, and after the laps, we drove the Elite into Amsterdam. That year, it was featured in a major article in Classic & Sports Car *magazine and also won 'Best Elite' at the Club Lotus autumn gathering at Stoneleigh.*

In 2003 it was back to France for the Club Lotus event at Château Tilques, and we took part in our first 'rally', a day-long navigation event around the lanes of Surrey, starting and finishing at Brooklands, with Paddy Hopkirk flagging us away. In 2004 the car was exhibited at the Classic Team Lotus fiftieth anniversary day at the factory in Hethel, where a couple of the workers from 1980 remembered the actual car and its special colour scheme. In the autumn of that year we took the car to Belgium, to take part in a meeting of classic British sports cars, and the car behaved impeccably as usual.

The car's highlights of 2005 were more laps of the Castle Combe circuit and a pre-Christmas trip to Le Touquet on the north French coast. In 2006, the Elite was chosen to be filmed for the Club Lotus 40th anniversary DVD, and we got to do some laps of the full Silverstone F1 circuit during the Retro-Run to the Silver-stone Classic, but even more fun were the laps of the Isle of Man TT circuit, after we joined a classic car tour of the island.

2007 was a terrific year for outings, as we did the Retro-Run again and also the newly reinstated MSA Classic, both events allowing the Elite to stretch its legs on some more laps of Silverstone, as well as the Millbrook and Longcross proving grounds. We also joined another classic car tour around the Ardennes mountains region on the Belgium/France border, taking in the old French Grand Prix circuit at Reims on the return journey. We were pleased to be invited by Lotus Cars Ltd to exhibit the Elite at the Hethel 40th celebrations, which was a fantastic event, and had us displayed alongside a spectacularly restored Essex Esprit Turbo. While we were queuing to get onto the test track in a convoy of cars built at Hethel, we noticed two young boys trying to cadge passenger rides, so when one of the boys got into an Elise ahead of us, we offered the other boy one of our rear seats, which he jumped into. One of the women with the two boys then told us that our new passenger was Magnus Chapman, son of Clive and grandson of Colin, sitting directly behind the seat that his grandfather had occupied some twenty-seven years earlier!

In 2008 we took the Elite up through Snowdonia to the Holyhead ferry, over to the east coast of Ireland for a tour that took in Dublin, the Mountains of Mourne, Belfast and the Giant's Causeway. The car also featured in Classic Cars magazine, and we had a fun photoshoot in the lanes near Silverstone, doing multi-car tracking shots in misty conditions. In 2009 and 2010, the car did not venture outside of England, but we enjoyed meeting other Elites and Eclats at the Lotus events in

Leigh has had the original Essex stickers that adorned the car back in the day reproduced.

Donington and Malvern, and convoys down to Castle Combe for some more laps of the circuit, as well as several classic car shows in the home counties. The Elite was treated to some specialist service at Paul Matty and at Lotus Bits, so it was ready to be the wedding transport for my cousin and his wife.

2011 was a busy year for the Elite, with four highlights. A south of England tour in April had the car speeding around the 'Alpine' route at Millbrook before ending up on the skidpan at the Porsche circuit at Silverstone. In May, we did a long loop through northern France, Belgium and Holland to meet up with an international group of Elite, Eclat and Excel owners for a weekend with Oliver Winter-

continued overleaf

Leigh Greenham's 1980 Elite Series 2.2 *continued*

The Elite is low and purposeful with a wide stance that displays purposefulness.

bottom, the cars' designer. An 800-mile trouble-free trip in four days. Then in June, the car was photographed and featured in *Classic & Sports Car* magazine, with the journalist preferring the Elite to the Mercedes and Lancia coupés that it was being compared with. Finally in November, the car was nominated for Classic Car of the Year, where it reached the top twenty in the online vote, and was on display at the NEC Classic Motor Show for three days. It was seen there by a Finnish photojournalist, who subsequently came to Oxfordshire for a photoshoot for the magazine *Mobilisti*.

We did our most ambitious journey in the Lotus in May 2012, driving down to the Monaco Historic Grand Prix, to recreate the photograph taken thirty-two years previously. We took four days to get there, travelling down the more western side of France, from Caen to Le Mans to the Loire Valley, the Dordogne, the Millau Viaduct, Nimes, through the Carmargue to Marseilles Airport, where we picked up two petrol-head chums. So, four-up, we cruised the final stage of the journey along the Provence autoroute, dropping down into Nice for the Promenade des Anglais, and on into Monaco, parking under the Hotel Columbus while the racing took place. After the racing, we were able to do several laps of the full circuit and visit the exact spot on the quayside where the car had been in the Lotus F1 paddock in 1980. We popped across the border into Italy, before taking a more central route through France, over the southern Alps, around the Gorges du Verdon, up past Orange, Lyon, several wine regions then into Belgium just in time to take part in the Ypres Lotus Day, with its tour around some nice Belgian countryside and villages. 2,200 miles in ten days.

The first weekend of 2013 saw us getting the Elite onto the Eurotunnel for a short trip to Paris, to join in a tour of the city's sites with over 600 other classic cars of all makes. Organized by a local car club, the tour was designed to gain publicity and protest at the Mairie de Paris plan to ban all old vehicles from the heart of the city. So we now have more photos of the car in famous foreign parts, including the Eiffel Tower, Moulin Rouge, Sacré Coeur, Montmartre, Notre Dame and Champs-Élysées. Then at August's Lotus Festival at Brands Hatch, the Elite was awarded second place in the Show and Shine competition. It was also exhibited at the two NEC Classic Car Shows in November 2013 and 2014.

So Leigh has not only rescued what is a historically significant car, he is also using it just as Lotus intended – as a high-speed, comfortable grand touring car, a role that it fulfils with ease and reliability.

CHAPTER TWO

DESIGN AND DEVELOPMENT OF THE LOTUS ELITE AND ECLAT

Despite building on the experience of producing the Elan, Plus 2 and Europa the Lotus four-seaters were innovative cars with their unsurpassed safety features, backbone chassis, striking looks and glass-fibre bodywork. They were regarded as being pretty exotic when they were first introduced, and seen as a viable British alternative to more exotic fare from Italy. The cars were especially well positioned thanks to the fuel crisis of 1974 when petrol prices went through the roof. The Elite and Eclat's 2-litre engine was smaller and more efficient than much of the opposition and, combined with the car's class-leading aerodynamics, gave much lower fuel costs than the performance of the car would suggest.

ENGINE – THE LOTUS 907 UNIT

The Lotus Type 75 Elite was powered by Lotus's first complete engine, the lightweight, all-alloy, 16-valve 907. The famous Lotus Twin Cam engine that had powered the Elan, Plus 2, Lotus Cortina and the Europa Twin Cam was essentially a Lotus-designed cylinder head on a Ford 116E block end. The 907 unit was a Lotus design through and through.

Early Development of the 900 Series

Lotus started to design the 907 in the late 1960s. Chapman's brief to his engineers laid down the engine's basic design parameters as 'high efficiency, flexibility, torque and smoothness which was suitable for hand assembly'. In addition to this brief, Lotus market and industry research resulted in

forward projections that showed the need for an engine that produced around 150bhp, had a low height to enable a low bonnet line, and was light. No such engine was available or in the pipeline of any manufacturer that Lotus could identify – although the Triumph Dolomite slant-4 was already in production for Saab – so the company decided to commence design work. With Steve Sanville heading up development and Ron Burr brought in from Coventry Climax, development was in safe hands. Tony Rudd took over development and productionizing of the design in the late 1960s.

The engine architecture was decided on as an all-alloy construction, 45-degree slant-4 (which allowed for the potential development of a 90-degree V8 unit which could be used for Indianapolis 500 racing), with belt-driven double overhead camshafts and 4 valves per cylinder. Initially development was concentrated on the cylinder head as Lotus knew this was the key to an engine's performance and with many of Lotus's engineers engaged on other work there were limited resources available for the new unit. As work progressed, Lotus became aware that General Motors' UK subsidiary, Vauxhall, was working on its own 2-litre, 4-cylinder, 45-degree-slant engine, which by coincidence shared the same bore centres. This meant Lotus could use the Vauxhall bottom end as a development mule while they designed the new cylinder head. This has led to rumours that the Lotus slant-4 unit was based on the Vauxhall engine but that is not the case.

As development continued, and to prove the proposed all-alloy engine's bottom end, Lotus

The first all-Lotus engine, the 900 series, was a 4-cylinder, dohc, 4-valve design. The cam belt is visible on this shot as the belt cover is missing. GROUP LOTUS PLC

The ancillaries were all driven off the front of the engine using V-belts – this unit only has an alternator, but a power steering pump and air conditioning compressor could also be fitted. GROUP LOTUS PLC

Yellow is the traditional Lotus colour. The colour emphasizes this Series I Elite's good looks.

designed and produced a pair of iron-block engines, types 904 and 905. The 904 was a 2-litre, fuel-injected race engine, marketed as the LV220 (LV standing for Lotus Vauxhall and the 220 being the claimed horsepower), with its inlet valves set at 41 degrees to the port and the ports enlarged – it was raced in the Group 6 Prototype-Sports Cars class in the two Lotus Type 62 cars, which were loosely based on the Europa, albeit with a new space-frame chassis and generally larger dimensions all round. The iron block used was originally from Vauxhall but when it developed cracks around the main bearing caps Lotus had a batch of reinforced engine blocks made which were used on all the 904 production engines.

The 905 was seen as a touring engine with a 51-degree inlet valve angle and standard sized ports. The 906 was intended to be a race engine with a sand-cast alloy crankcase, while the 907 was the first production road engine, which used an all die-cast alloy block assembly and the 51-degree valve angle. The 907 was destined to first appear in the new Jensen-Healey in 1972.

Prior to this, 900-series engines had been tested on the road from 1968 in a Vauxhall Viva GT (registered to Lotus as RAH 713F) and a Bedford CF van, Vauxhall's commercial division's competitor for the more popular Ford Transit. Having some 150bhp in either of these vehicles must have come as a surprise to other drivers at the time! The van was used as a general delivery vehicle by the factory. This was another example of Chapman's love of getting things to do more than one job: Lotus could test the engine(s) in the real world while delivering spares to dealers and picking up components from suppliers. The van did have a tendency to destroy transmissions and rear tyres and wear out brake linings in no time, but it covered some 136,700 miles (220,000 km) with the engines installed.

The 908 and 909 versions of the engine were V8s (908 for racing and 909 for road use) and one was built in 1984 for the Etna concept car, but, as usual, the money ran out before it could be put into production. Lotus did finally make a production V8 engine, which was fitted in the Esprit from 1996 onwards, but this was a completely new design.

Design and Layout of the 907 Unit

The final design of the all-alloy road or tourer 907 unit used in the Elite family and the Jensen-Healey resulted in a 1973cc 4-cylinder, in-line unit with the cylinder bores mounted at 45 degrees. The engine used metric dimensions and thread forms, apart from the Zenith Stromberg carburettors used on the 'Federal' (i.e. US) engines, the oil filter and the alternator which used Unified (UNF and UNC) thread forms. The cylinder head, block and sump were all gravity die-cast in LM 25-TF aluminium alloy. Rather than having five separate bearing caps, as in more conventional engine designs, the 900 had a one-piece carrier for all five lower halves of the main bearings giving a single casting that integrated the five main bearing caps. This approach was adopted to make it easier for the foundry to produce the raw engine casings, removing as it did the need to machine out deep main bearing saddles which would have needed substantial broaching equipment.

The crankcase was split along the crankshaft centre line and the one-piece aluminium alloy bearing housing was fitted between the sump and the centre line of the crankcase and fixed in position around its perimeter with ten nuts and washers where it formed the lower outer wall or skirt of the crankcase. The bearing carrier was accurately located to the crankcase upper using a pair of dowels. The main bearings were held in place by a further ten studs that ran from the 'top' crankcase through the bearing carrier and were fixed in place with nuts and washers. The whole assembly was line bored in one piece to ensure accurate alignment of the top and bottom main bearing shells. The sump was bolted to the bearing carrier and had a bolt-on anti-surge plate. The cylinder bores were formed using cast-iron wet liners, which were designed to sit slightly proud of the block's top deck by approximately 0.1 to 0.15mm, with the cylinder head gasket taking up the gap. The crankshaft was cast in SNG 37/2 iron, and was supported on the five split shell main bearings. Thrust washers were fitted to the main bearing at the flywheel end.

Connecting rods were aluminium alloy (EN16) with split-shell, big-end bearings located by dowels. Both the main and big end bearing shells were

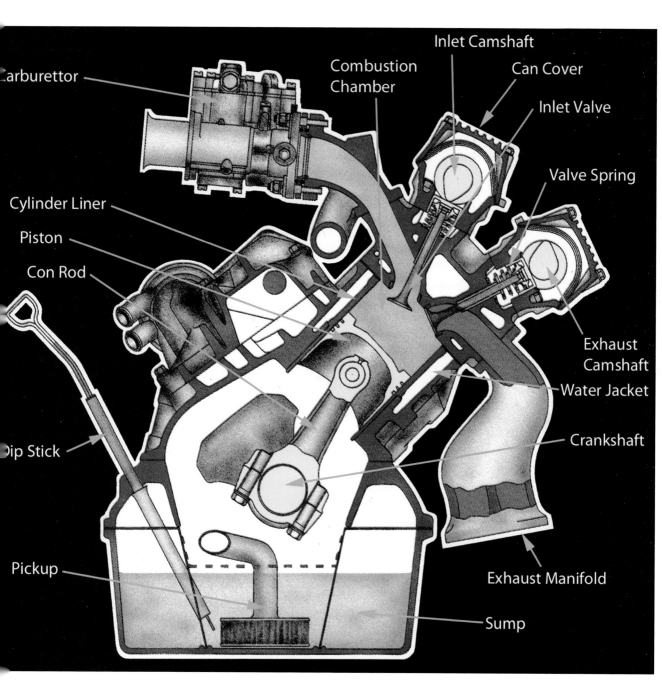

A cross section of the 900 series unit shows salient points and the architecture of the engine. GROUP LOTUS PLC

The crankcases were made up in a sandwich, split along the centre of the main bearings. The bearing shell lower carriers were incorporated into the lower crankcase casting as shown here.
GROUP LOTUS PLC

made from Vandervell VP/2 copper-lead composite alloy. The small end bearing was a pressed in bronze bush. The oil pump and distributor were mounted in an auxiliary casting bolted to the top face of the crankcase, which also carried the canister-type oil filter. The oil pump and distributor were driven directly by a jack shaft which was in turn driven from a dedicated toothed pulley, identical to the pair of camshaft drive pulleys, and driven from the timing belt at the front of the engine. As a result the distributor and oil filter faced backwards and were hidden under the carburettors, making access awkward, which as the distributor carried contact breaker points was not very convenient for the poor mechanic who needed to adjust them. Electronic ignition with Lumenition optical pickup replacing the points was fitted to later engines. The water pump was housed in a casting bolted to the front of the engine and driven by a V-belt from the nose of the crank which was shared with the alternator.

Pistons were light alloy with indents for all four valves and were flat topped for high-compression motors and dished for low-compression (Federal) engines. The cylinder head was, like the crankcase,

gravity die-cast in LM 25-TF aluminium alloy and had four valves per cylinder, with a 38-degree angle between the inlet and exhaust valves. A single 14mm spark plug was centrally mounted for each cylinder and the combustion chamber was hemispherical. Valve seats were Brico sintered inserts, the valve guides were cast iron and double valve springs were employed. The head gasket was a composite asbestos and stainless steel item, and the exhaust manifold was a cast-iron, four-into-two unit, with a flanged plate connecting to a two-branch downpipe which was joined to the exhaust system by a Y-pipe.

The two cast-iron camshafts were both mounted in a pair of alloy camshaft carriers which bolted to the top of the cylinder head. Bucket tappets were used to operate the valves, with clearance being maintained with shims. Both inlet and exhaust camshafts were identical and were driven by a toothed belt from the crankshaft nose. The belt was tensioned using a spring-loaded idler wheel and the belt also drove the distributor and oil pump through a third sprocket. On the later Federal cars the back of the belt was used to drive the emissions air pump. Each cam was covered by a cast alloy cover which was fixed in place using a thick gasket and ten perimeter bolts and had strengthening ribs and the Lotus name cast in the top to make the engine both more attractive and recognizable. The flywheel was a steel unit and carried an 8-in diameter single plate clutch which was cable operated.

The Elite's exhaust system was a three-box system, starting from the manifold on the left-hand side of the car with a pair of pipes that merged into one just behind the engine. This pipe fed into a single silencer mounted centrally under the passenger compartment. Two pipes came out of the central silencer, each one branching outwards, looping over the driveshafts and connecting to a final large-diameter silencer. The silencers were positioned off-centre on either side of the car to give the rear a neat, balanced look. The subdued note of the exhaust met all noise legislation.

Ancillaries were driven from a number of V-belts from the crankshaft nose. There could be up to three belts driven from a pulley on the crankshaft nose; all engines had the alternator and water pump

An external toothed belt was used to drive the camshafts. Here it is on a 2.2-litre 912 unit.

driven by the first belt. Cars with power steering had a second V-belt to drive the power steering pump, while cars with power steering and air conditioning had a third belt to drive the condenser.

Engine by Lotus – Development by Customers

The first production 907 engines were fitted to the Jensen-Healey and tests of pre-production cars threw up some issues. The pre-production engines had their sumps cut and welded to fit in the Healey, and had tubular exhaust manifolds.

Initial Testing

While the performance of the engine was as expected, the initial testing of the engines in the prototype Jensen-Healey cars revealed vibration, which was a result of the beam stiffness of the engine gearbox assembly being suspect. This issue seemed to have been caused by a combination of the cut and shut sumps and general lack of stiffness in the engine's cases. The solution was to add an additional pair of gearbox locating lugs to the crankcases which, when the gearbox was firmly bolted into place, helped to solve the issue.

A further three issues arose when the cars were close to production – all oil system related. When the engine was cruised above 6,000rpm oil was being ingested into the air box through the breathing system, resulting in the oil being burnt, resulting in a shortage of oil and rapidly diminishing oil pressure. Initially an oil separator was fitted to the breather to return the oil to the sump before it got into the air box; a permanent cure was to modify the engine's internal breather system by using the

The Lotus 907 engine was first used in the Jensen-Healey – a two-seat, open-topped sports car.

crankcase's front oil seal holder as an oil separation chamber, ensuring that the oil was not ingested into the breathing system in the first place.

It was found that a second factor causing low oil pressure was inadequate drainage from the cylinder head back down into the sump, leading to the oil level in the sump being reduced and the oil pressure dropping. This was found to be caused by mismatched drain holes and casting flash obscuring some drains. As these were assembly and machining issues rather than fundamental design flaws, they were relatively easy to fix. Finally, incorrectly sized oil pressure relief valves caused delays in the engine's oil pressure getting to an acceptable level from start-up, which was solved by making sure the pressure release valves were correctly sized.

Launch of the Jensen-Healey

The new Jensen Healey was announced to the press in March 1972. It was favourably received and had good initial road tests – although some test cars had a bit of a thirst for oil. Long-term tests of the Jensen-Healey run by the UK's motoring press resulted in *Autocar* headlining their review 'Engine by Lotus; Gearbox by Chrysler; Suspension by Vauxhall; Development by customers?' as a result of a large number of problems, including high oil consumption, resulting in two engine changes under warranty. Finally the replacement of the oil control rings for a better designed variant resulted in an acceptable level of oil consumption. Other issues with the engine on early cars included general oil leaks

**In the Jensen-Healey the engine, after some initial problems, proved to be a strong performer.
Note the 'Jensen-Healey' name cast into the camshaft covers.**

and suspect beam rigidity resulting in irritating vibration and harshness.

In late 1973 the Jensen-Healey Mk II was introduced. This had a significantly improved engine with redesigned crankcases which cured a lot of the original unit's oil leaks and stiffened the cases to cut down on vibration and harshness. Later cars were also fitted with the Getrag five-speed gearbox later seen on the Elite.

The reputation of the Jensen-Healey suffered badly from these early problems with the engine and various other issues around the build quality. Sales were disappointing, with just over 10,000 cars being delivered between 1972 and 1976, and a lot of blame for the poor sales can be laid on the underdeveloped Lotus engine. By the time the Mk

II Jensen-Healey was in production in August 1973 the engine was genuinely a good unit but unfortunately mud sticks and the Jensen-Healey never managed to shrug off the poor reputation of the first production models. The story of the Jensen-Healey was a typical example of a manufacturer bringing an underdeveloped product to market, and in the Jensen-Healey's case their main market for the car was the United States – which was (and is) notoriously unforgiving of such actions.

What was bad news for Jensen was good for Lotus. Production of the 907 unit for Jensen enabled Lotus to get its new engine production plant up and running. With the teething problems of the 907 unit sorted out during the supply of engines to Jensen, along with the ongoing development of the

EXPANSION AT HETHEL

In order to produce the new engine, Lotus invested heavily (to the tune of some £500,000) in building a new engine production facility at the Hethel works. The facility utilized 'numerically controlled' plant – the forerunner to today's Computer Numerically Controlled (CNC) machine tools – to machine the die-cast aluminium components (the crankcase, bearing cover, sump, cylinder head and cam carriers), turning them from raw die-castings to finished pieces.

The plant comprised a pair of Marwin Max-E-Mill twin-spindle, vertical, heavy-duty milling, drilling, boring and tapping machines and a Min-E-Centre travelling-column, heavy-duty machining centre which was equipped with a Plessey electronic control system. Initial work on castings, comprising face milling, boring and tapping holes, was carried out on the Min-E-Centre, and final work on castings was then carried out on the Max-E-Mills, one working on the crankcases, the other on the cylinder heads. In addition the facility utilized Moog machining centres, line-boring machines and Cintimatic machining centres to carry out further operations on castings and ancillary engine components.

At the time the facility was installed (early 1972) it was the first one in the UK to produce engines completely by using numerically controlled machines. Another element of the facility was its flexibility; if components needed to be altered, for example to meet changes required as a result of changes to emissions legislation, the facility just needed to modify the machine's data input to execute any required changes.

Lotus invested heavily in computer-controlled machines to process the engine's raw die-castings. Here two crankcases are being machined. GROUP LOTUS PLC

CAMSHAFT SPECIFICATIONS

European and Federal camshaft opening and closing degrees are given in the following table:

	European camshaft	Federal camshaft
Lift	0.36in (0.9144cm)	0.25in (0.635cm)
Inlet opens	25 degrees BTDC	26 degrees BTDC
Inlet closes	65 degrees ATDC	66 degrees ATDC
Exhaust opens	65 degrees BTDC	66 degrees BTDC
Exhaust closes	25 degrees ATDC	26 degrees ATDC

[ATDC: After Top Dead Centre – BTDC: Before Top Dead Centre]

907 unit while fitted to the Jensen-Healey, Lotus were confident that they had a tried-and-tested unit when the Elite was launched.

The Elite's Engines

The first production motors for the Elite were produced in two forms – one for the United States (Federal version) and one for the UK and the rest of the world (European version). The latter came with a 9.5:1 compression ratio and a pair of 45mm twin-choke Dellorto DHLA 45E carburettors. Lotus was used to the Dellorto carburettor having used them on the later Elans to replace the more expensive twin-choke Webbers and the less sporting looking Strombergs. The European engines gave a claimed 160bhp at 6,500rpm and 140lb ft of torque at 5,000rpm. Federal versions had slightly different cam profiles, a compression ratio of 8.4:1 and a pair of Stromberg 175 CD-2SE carburettors. Again, Lotus had a good deal of experience of the Stromberg CD carburettor as it had been used on the federal versions of the Twin Cam engine fitted to the Elans destined for the United States, and was fitted as standard across the Elan range for a while. The Strombergs were responsible for the 'power bulge' seen on the later Elans and, although not favoured by the racing fraternity, on the Lotus Twin Cam engine the pair of Stromberg carburettors gave practically the same power with better emissions performance and less fussy running than the Webbers.

When fitted to the Federal specification 907 unit the combination of the twin Stromberg carburettors, lower compression ratio and softer cam profiles gave a slightly lower output with a claimed 140bhp at 6,600rpm and 130lb ft of torque at 5,000rpm.

The Lotus 912 Engine

Introduced in the Series 2.2 Elite and Eclat in 1980, the 2172cc 912 engine was a development of the 907 engine and was primarily designed to give more torque than the 907 unit. By the late 1970s the market had changed and although the 907 had broadly met Chapman's original brief to be highly efficient, flexibly, torquey and smooth, there was room for improvement and a need to meet new requirements to produce more torque and improved fuel economy. The basic architecture and structure of the new unit remained the same as the 907, but an increase in the stroke to 76.2mm (from the 907 unit's 69.2mm) gave a capacity of 2172cc, up 199cc from the 907's 1973cc, and the compression ratio was 9.44:1 – slightly lower than the 907's 9.5:1.

The 2.2 912 unit was developed from the 911 unit as fitted to the Sunbeam/Talbot Lotus of 1979, but was significantly different in detail, including new camshafts, oil sump, cylinder head and main bear-

The 2.2 version of the 900 series engine was developed from the unit fitted to the Talbot/Sunbeam Lotus. Externally there were few clues to the increase in torque or capacity. GROUP LOTUS PLC

ing castings. The increased capacity resulted in a significant boost to the engine's peak torque, up to 160lb ft at 5,000rpm, as opposed to the 907's 140lb ft at 5,000rpm. Significantly the 912 unit produced 140lb ft of torque, the 907's peak torque output, at a mere 2,400rpm. Peak power from the 912 remained at 160bhp, and was produced at 6,500rpm.

As with the later 907 units, Lotus fitted Lumenition contactless ignition to all 912s which improved matters from a maintainability perspective. Redesigned camshaft carriers and revised cam covers were fitted to help cure the original camshaft covers' habit of leaking oil. With the introduction of

the 912 unit, the Borg Warner Type 65 automatic gearbox torque converter and valve body assembly were modified to match the new torque characteristics of the new engine.

The 912 engine was carried forward unchanged from the Elite and Eclat Series 2.2 into the Excel. In October 1985 the SE Excel was introduced with a revised 912 unit which was tuned to give 180bhp at 6,500rpm along with 150lb ft of torque at 5,250rpm.

The major change on paper to produce the SE variant of the 912 was the increasing of the compression ratio to 10.9:1, but that was only part of the story. The inlet and exhaust ports in the cylin-

The 180bhp SE variant had new cam covers with the fins picked out in red.

der head were modified to improve gas flow, and a new camshaft, derived from those developed for the Talbot competitions department and used on the Talbot/Sunbeam Lotus, was specified. This camshaft gave longer opening of the inlet and exhaust valves. While the valve sizes and combustion chamber shape remained unchanged, new Mahle forged alloy pistons, with short skirts and a crown raised by 1mm, were used to provide the increase in compression ratio. The new pistons ran in new cylinder liners, made from forged alloy with a hard Nikasil coating to resist wear.

The SE also featured revised Dellorto carburettors, type DHLA 45D, which featured a third jet (in addition to the standard pilot and main jets) that came into use at high revs to give a better fuel-air mixture throughout the rev range. The SE engine was finished off with new cam covers, which were stiffer and had the fins and Lotus name backing picked out in red paint.

TRANSMISSION

Clutch

The Elite's clutch was a conventional 8½in-diameter, single-plate unit, cable operated and cased in an alloy bell housing. Operation was by cable, with a small-diameter wheel placed in the pedal box to guide the cable from the foot pedal lever around to the bell housing. This mechanism made replacing a clutch cable awkward, and also forced the cable round a tighter diameter than was optimal which contributed to shortening the life of the cable.

Gearbox

Manual

The Elite was introduced with the Lotus five-speed manual gearbox first used on the Elan Plus 2. The box used Austin Maxi internals which were housed in a Lotus-designed, all-alloy casting. Gear ratios were first 3.2:1; second 2.01:1; third 1.37:1; fourth 1.00:1; and overdrive fifth 0.80:1. While the box performed relatively well in the smaller and lighter Plus 2, it gained a reputation for fragility when used in the heavier and more powerful Elite. Initial reports of its performance indicated that the gate was narrow and gear lever travel short and

that the change was generally good and the action smooth. However some reports showed that the synchromesh between fourth and third was weak, and the box could baulk when selecting reverse. In one long-term test the gearbox did fail, with the loss of teeth from the third gear pinion along with deteriorating first gear synchromesh at around 27,000 miles (43,500km).

In general it was found that over time the gearbox was the weakest link in the Elite's powertrain with rebuilds being necessary after around 40–50,000 miles (65–80,000km) of average usage. The Lotus five-speed gearbox, with its Austin Maxi-derived internals, was eventually superseded by a German-sourced Getrag five-speed box, which was fitted to the Series 2.2 cars; the Getrag was replaced with a Toyota five-speed box for the Eclat Excel. The drive was taken from the gearbox to the differential by a tubular propshaft, with two Hardy Spicer type universal joints, two rubber sleeves to absorb torsional forces and a sliding spine fitment at the gearbox.

Automatic

The Elite 504 automatic gearbox option was announced at the October 1975 London Earls Court Motor Show, and the Eclat 524 automatic option was announced in early 1976. When speci-

The Lotus five-speed gearbox was assembled in-house using Lotus castings and Austin Maxi gears. GROUP LOTUS PLC

**The Lotus five-speed gearbox proclaimed its manufacturer to the world
with 'Lotus' cast into the alloy case.**

fied with an automatic gearbox, the Elite and Eclat used the ubiquitous Borg Warner BW65 unit. While the Borg Warner BW35 box was initially documented as being fitted, it appears that only the BW65 was used. The unit had three forward speeds and reverse and was hydraulically controlled with torque converter. It was an option on many British cars of the time, including the Triumph Stag, Dolomite and 2000, the MGB, and various Jaguars, Fords and Rovers. The box was originally designed in the United States for smaller-engined cars with engine capacity under 200cu in or 3300cc but it was also suitable for larger European cars of around the same capacity.

The box was operated using a T-lever on the centre console utilizing a dog-leg gate to select the various functions of (from front to back) park, reverse, neutral, drive, second and first. The selector was connected to a lever on the gearbox side by an adjustable rod, and the gearbox had an electric interlock system that only allowed the starter to operate when the box was in park or neutral. The three gears gave a range of ratios – top could operate between 3.70:1 to 8.41:1; second 5.37:1 to 12.20:1 and first 8.85:1 to 20.14:1. Reverse gave 7.75:1 to 17.62:1.

The base model Eclat (the 520, also known as the Sprint in the US market) was equipped with a four-speed Ford gearbox, based on that used in the then current Granada. While it lacked the overdrive top gear of the Lotus five-speed gearbox it was generally well received as it had an excellent shift action, well-chosen ratios and was robust and reliable.

Series 2.2

With the Series 2.2 Elite a German Getrag five-speed manual gearbox was specified. The use of a proprietary unit was driven by the relatively low numbers of cars being produced, which meant the high-quality German box was cheaper to purchase direct than it was for Lotus to make their own, sometimes troubled unit. The Getrag box had five forward gears, all with synchromesh and had ratios of first 2.96:1; second 1.93:1; third 1.39:1; fourth 1.00:1; and fifth 0.813:1 – a slightly closer set of ratios than the original Lotus box. Coupled with a higher final gear ratio in the differential of 4.0:1 this box overcame the reliability issues experienced with the original Lotus five-speed unit.

Final Drive

The Elite's rear differential was a conventional Salisbury 7HA unit with hypoid gears, and was supplied in two ratios, 3.73:1 or 4.1:1. The unit was rubber mounted onto the chassis, and the casing was adapted to fit the Elite and Eclat's inboard drum brakes. The rubber mounts had to be relatively resilient as the rear suspension loads were fed into the differential through the driveshafts, so there was a loss of refinement as noise and vibration could be transmitted into the chassis. This issue persisted until the introduction of the revised rear suspension on the Excel, when the driveshafts did not take any suspension loads so the differential mounting rubbers could be softer. The differential was changed to a Toyota supplied unit at this time.

The use of inboard rear drums mounted close to the differential casing did raise some questions about heat soak from the brakes into the differential but did not seem to be an issue with most owners. A more common problem was the failure of the rear differential output shaft seals which resulted in differential oil leaking out and contaminating the rear brakes.

CHASSIS DESIGN

Monocoque versus Backbone

At first glance it appears that the Elite reused the backbone chassis and glass-fibre bodyshell concept proven in the Elan and Plus 2. While this is true, the Elite's architecture was arrived at in a roundabout way. Originally, when the design

of the Elite was started, Lotus looked closely at the use of a glass-fibre monocoque as seen in the original Elite (Model 14). This approach was also initially pursued in the design of the Elan, but the Elan's open top robbed the proposed monocoque of too much strength, so the backbone chassis was adopted; initially as a development mule, and finally as the basis for production. With the new Elite being a two-door four-seater with a roof, the use of a glass-fibre monocoque was an obvious concept to look into as although larger it was essentially the same format as the original Elite and the roof gave the design potential to be a true glass-fibre monocoque.

The advantages of a monocoque construction (even in glass fibre) over a separate chassis were understood at Lotus. A properly designed monocoque offered lightness, strength and stiffness, as well as being inherently cost-effective and (if built in glass fibre) rustproof and innovative, all core Lotus values. However, as the design of the Elite progressed the need for a pair of steel subframes to support the engine, drive and suspension became apparent. A steel subframe front and rear was easy to make and took a lot of the major localized stresses away from the shell, meaning it could be lighter, and it was easier to make accurately and bolt to the body, rather than trying to accurately bond metal reinforcements into the body. The weight gained by using a pair of subframes was countered by the need for less glass fibre in the shell, and as the cost of resin had gone up in line with the sharp rise in the price of oil in the early 1970s, the subframes probably were cheaper to make than using additional glass fibre and resin.

As the concept was developed the temptation to join the front and rear subframes with a steel structure became compelling – not only did it add stiffness to the car and hence took away the need for reinforcing in the shell, but it also meant that it was relatively easy to ensure the front and rear suspension was in alignment and not dependent on the accurate moulding of the bodyshell – and moulding a glass-fibre bodyshell was, at the time, still more of an art than a science and subject to lots of influences that could result in minor but significant changes between supposedly identical

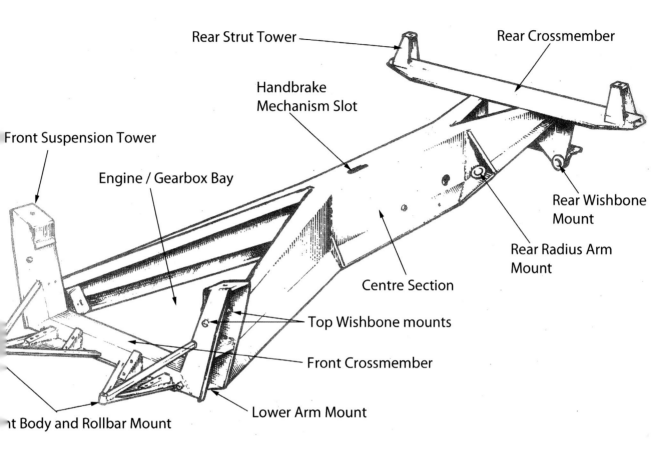

Rear Strut Tower

Rear Crossmember

Handbrake
Mechanism Slot

Front Suspension Tower

Engine / Gearbox Bay

Rear Wishbone
Mount

Rear Radius Arm
Mount

Centre Section

Top Wishbone mounts

Front Crossmember

Lower Arm Mount

nt Body and Rollbar Mount

**The Elite's backbone chassis was made from folded-steel sheet,
and was light and strong.** GROUP LOTUS PLC

shells. The additional weight of a steel connecting structure also meant there was less glass fibre and resin needed in the body to make it stiffer. So in a somewhat roundabout way the Elite ended up with a pressed-steel backbone chassis, very similar in concept to the Elan, but described by Lotus at the time as a 'pair of interconnected subframes'.

Chassis Construction
The Elite's chassis was made from folded sheet steel and was very similar in outline (if not in detail) to the Elan chassis. The Elite chassis was approximately 124in (3,158mm) long, the front cross member was 40in (1,025mm) wide, and the rear cross member was 44in (1,126mm) wide. The chassis comprised a front V-shaped section to take the engine and gearbox with turrets

mounted on each side of the front cross member to mount the front suspension. The front suspension fulcrum points were removable bolts to enable easy repair after minor accidents (on the Elan the fulcrums were welded onto the chassis making repairs after a minor shunt disproportionally expensive). Unlike the previous generation of Elans, the chassis front cross member was not used as a reservoir for the headlight vacuum system. Forwards of the front cross member, a pair of V-shaped extensions, fabricated from steel tube and sheet, were used to support the nose of the car and provide attachment for the front bumper and radiator. The centre section was a large rectangular box section, approximately 43in (110cm) long, 11.5in (29cm) wide and 11in (28cm) in height, inside which ran the propeller shaft. At the rear, the chassis terminated in a cross section that ran across the width of the car and carried the differential and rear suspension pick-up points.

The chassis was painted and was, unfortunately, not particularly rust resistant; later chassis (from around 1980 and the Series 2.2 cars) were galvanized (as were replacement units) and offered much better rust resistance. The chassis was quite rigid torsionally, with a stiffness of 1,800lb/ft per degree of movement. With the body mounted the torsional stiffness of the whole car increased to 2,000lb/ft per degree.

SUSPENSION

The Lotus Elite was a radical departure from the past for Lotus. The car was a true four-seater, with space for four adults and reasonable luggage space, but it aimed to provide the buyer with all the convenience and comfort of a true GT car with the handling and performance of a Lotus sports car. When the Elan was designed, the traditional British sports car approach to suspension was to limit wheel travel and use stiff springing, but the Elan was designed according to Lotus and Chapman's modern approach to handling and roadholding, relying on long wheel travel, relatively soft springs and well controlled damping and roll. As a result the Elan and Plus 2 were widely praised for their compliant and comfortable ride allied to impeccable handling and roadholding.

It was a logical move to build on this experience to provide a similar ride in the Elite. This meant that the Elite had to have independent suspension at both ends, and would need to have adequate wheel travel to soak up road imperfections. An important factor in the front and rear suspension design was the use of carefully chosen rubber bushing to influence each wheel's behaviour and travel as it was deflected. In the case of the rear suspension, the bushings actually contributed positively to the car's handling by allowing a carefully controlled amount of self steering, provided by the rubber mounting of the front of the radius arm. The toe-in of the rear wheels was also adjustable by using shims on the mounting pads of the radius arm rubber mounts where they were bolted to the chassis.

Front Suspension

The Elite's front suspension looked to modern practice and in Chapman's usual manner used conventional components in unconventional ways. The front suspension comprised a top wishbone and a lower single U-section link. The top wishbone was made up of two U-section channels, which were pivoted on the chassis on metalastic bushes. The lower link was pivoted on the chassis with a single metalastic bush and located using an anti-roll bar, which joined the lower links of both sides and twisted on conventional rubber bushes fitted into carriers bolted onto the chassis. A ball joint was bolted to the end of the top wishbone and fixed with a taper joint to a forged steel upright, and the lower link used a Triumph Herald-type trunnion to mount the bottom of the upright. Front suspension movement was controlled by a coilover damper unit which was bolted to the lower link and passed between the two top wishbone sections to a top mounting on the chassis. The front upright was broadly speaking the same as that used on the Elan (being derived from the Triumph Herald/Spitfire/GT6 component) and pivoted on the threaded lower trunnion and upper ball joint to allow for steering movement.

The lower trunnion was made from cast bronze and had two functions – it allowed the upright to swivel to give steering and it allowed the lower link to articulate independently of the upright, allowing the suspension to move up and down. The steering movement was achieved by having the upright threaded into the trunnion using a coarse thread which allowed the upright to turn and gave plenty of bearing surface. Lotus recommended filling the trunnion with gearbox oil on a regular basis to avoid the trunnion seizing on the upright (a not uncommon occurrence on any vehicle using the Triumph trunnion), resulting at best in heavy steering and at worst in the threaded part of the upright snapping – causing the front wheel to splay out and the car to come to a rapid halt.

Suspension movement was achieved using a pair of large-diameter, top-hat shaped nylon bushes placed in housing on the back of the trunnion. The trunnion was bolted onto the end of the lower link using a bolt through the nylon bushes. A

**The Elite's front suspension used twin upper wishbones and single lower link
the solid disc rotor was gripped by a twin opposed piston caliper.**

tubular metal sleeve was fitted between the bolt and the bushes, and the through bolt clamped this sleeve between the sides of the U-section link. This acted to isolate the bushes from the clamping bolt, allowing the trunnion to pivot around the nylon bushes to cater for the suspension movement. This sleeve is notorious for seizing to the bolt, making it difficult to renew the bushes; however, a seized bolt did not affect the suspension movement as the upright pivoted on the bushes, it just made it extremely difficult to remove the bolt if the bushes needed to be replaced – copious amounts of suitable grease on the bolt is recommended to stave off corrosion.

A pair of pressed-steel plates and a sealing rubber was used to keep the weather out of the assembly. The combined steering arm and brake caliper bracket was bolted onto the upright, and the front wheel's stub axle was bolted into position in the middle of the upright on a taper. The front suspension gave $3^5/_8$in (92mm) bump and $3\frac{1}{2}$in (89mm) of rebound, giving $7^1/_8$in (181mm) of travel. Four bolts fixed the front brake discs to the hub, which was mounted on the stub axle on the upright with an adjustable taper roller wheel bearing outboard and a conventional roller bearing inboard. The hub was fixed to the stub axle with a castellated nut.

With the caliper removed, the top swivel joint and lower Triumph-sourced trunnion can be seen.

Rear Suspension

At the rear of the car the suspension was slightly less conventional. The independent suspension used the driveshaft as an upper link and had a tubular lower link. A sheet-steel radius arm completed the three suspension elements.

The rear hub carrier was a substantial alloy casting and was bolted to the lower link and the radius arm using a long fore and aft stud, while a transverse stud carried the coilover damper unit and

ran from the front of the hub carrier, through the damper's bottom eye and passed through the rear face of the radius arm. The driveshaft incorporated a pair of universal joints and was bolted through the brake drum onto a drive plate at the differential end and to a flange on the outer driveshaft which was located in the hub carrier.

The rear suspension had a number of subtle features in its design. The cast-alloy hub carrier – and hence the hub and wheel – were kept at a

At the rear of the car, looking from the rear, the driveshaft provided a top link, while a tubular lower link joined the hub carrier to the chassis. Coilover shock absorbers provided springing and damping.

Visible on this rotted out chassis – note the top cross member – are the inboard drum brakes and the large triangular radius arm, with its front mount on the side of the chassis.

constant angle to the road and the vehicle axis through the bottom mount, a fore and aft pin. The spring and damper lower mountings were located on an offset side-to-side stud which was designed to make the spring and damper assembly slightly skewed in relation to the suspension movement. This meant that when the suspension moved the damper was not in line with suspension movement, and this induced twisting which the trailing arm had to take up via the arm itself flexing and movement in its flexible front mounting. This resulted in a progressive stiffening of the suspension as the suspension approached its limits.

The rear suspension gave 4in (102mm) bump and 3½in (89mm) of rebound, giving 7½in (190mm) of travel.

BRAKES, STEERING AND WHEELS

Brakes

The Elite's brakes were not quite state of the art supercar specification, comprising front discs and rear drums – a fairly mundane set-up seen on most mid-range family cars in the 1970s. The Elite's front brakes were 10.44 x 0.5in solid discs, gripped by Girling opposed piston calipers. Each caliper actually had three pistons – two small-diameter ones on the outside edge and a single larger-diameter one on the inside to give adequate running clearance for the alloy wheels.

What was interesting – and probably unique to the Elite at the time – was the use of inboard rear drums, which were primarily designed to reduce the unsprung weight of the rear suspension components. The brake drums were 9 x 2.25in cast-iron units, with single leading shoe activation and automatic adjustment. The handbrake operated on the rear drums via cable-operated levers incorporated into the drum mechanism. This set-up remained broadly unchanged up to the introduction of the Excel, although the base model Eclat 520 had smaller front discs (Triumph GT6 type as used on the last Elan Plus 2) and smaller twin-piston calipers.

Steering

Steering of the Elite and Eclat was by a Burman-made rack-and-pinion system, with three turns lock to lock. The power-steering option used a V-belt-driven pump mounted on the engine and a lower-geared Burman rack and pinion giving three and a half turns lock to lock. The power steering was universally criticized by the press at the time for being too light; however, this was a criticism levelled at virtually every GT car with power steering at the time and as time has progressed and power steering has become the norm the Elite's system was nowhere near as bad as the press claimed.

Wheels

The Elite was equipped with 14in-diameter dished pressure die-cast alloy wheels as standard, a design unique to the Elite and produced by GKN. Held onto the hub with four studs with countersunk nuts to locate them, the wheels featured an inner dish with a series of twelve cooling slots between the inner dish and the rim. The inner dish, rim and the rear face of the wheel was machined smooth to aid balancing; at the front, the whole face of the wheel was polished. The wheels were finished with an electrostatic applied acrylic coating to ensure corrosion resistance. Special 205/60 VR x 14 tyres were developed by Dunlop for the Elite, which were optimized to work with and enhance the Elite's suspension. Later on Goodyear also provided tyres to Lotus.

BODY

Bodyshell

Fibreglass Moulding Techniques

Glass fibre mass-production techniques were well established by the early 1970s and usually comprised the use of hydraulic presses and steel moulds to form relatively small and simple parts out of premade and precut Sheet Moulding Compound (SMC). SMC was a resin and glass-fibre matting sandwich, made by spreading the required amount of resin on a plastic film, spray-

The Series I Elites (and Eclats) were fitted with this type of GKN alloy wheel.

ing glass fibre onto the resin, then placing another plastic film with resin on it onto the chopped strand to form a sandwich of plastic film, resin, chopped strand glass fibre, resin and plastic film. The resin mix would be quite 'stiff' and the SMC would normally be made up as a long 'roll' in a continuous process. The SMC resin would have a heat-sensitive catalyst incorporated in it, and the SMC could be premade, stored and cut to shape before being placed on the mould.

The heat-sensitive catalyst meant the SMC would stay uncured until it was heated up to a critical temperature, usually in the mould while in the press. This technique resulted in very strong mouldings that were properly cured throughout and needed little if any rectification apart from de-flashing the cured mouldings. The technique also had very little wastage of resin and glass fibre, and it was easy to incorporate different strengths or thicknesses of SMC in different parts of the mould as needed. The finished part would have no exposed matting and a smooth finish on both sides.

The disadvantage of this type of production was the investment required in proper metal tooling for the moulds; plant to produce consistent SMC; and the large and expensive combined hydraulic presses and curing heaters. Hence most makers of large glass-fibre items, such as boats and car bodies, still tended to use hand lay-up techniques married to multi-piece, 'bolt-together' moulds. Chapman recognized the advantages of the semi-automated press system over the traditional hand lay-up methods used on the previous Elite and the Elan, and he wanted to get away from the Elan's complex multi-part, bolt-together moulds. Multi-piece moulds were needed to accommodate the

The Series 2 Elites gained these 'Lotus' branded alloy wheels produced by Speedline.

The interior of the Elite was relatively roomy. The Eclat and Excel's cut down rear roof did reduce headroom for back seat passengers. GROUP LOTUS PLC

Elan's curves, especially the 'tumble-home' found on the front and rear wings.

'Tumble-home' is a term used to describe the inward curve towards the centre line on a car's (or boat's) front and rear sides – if the mould for an Elan's one-piece bodyshell were produced in one piece then it would be impossible to get the shell out of the mould. In addition, hand laying up of complex moulds was a skilled job if it was to be done correctly and the joints in the mould that allowed it to be dismantled always left lines in the gel coat that would need rectification. The hand lay-up process also relied on the proper mixing of the resin and catalyst and careful placing of the matt and any reinforcing elements and thorough stippling of the resin into the matt. Not only was the process very labour intensive, it was also messy: the

shells had exposed matt on the sides that weren't to the mould, giving an unfinished look, and the finished shells usually needed lots of rectification before they could be used.

Customizing the Process

Chapman was looking to a more efficient process to produce the bodies for his new upmarket car. He wanted to get away from the kit-car image, which meant he needed to have no exposed matt and a good-quality finish. He also wanted the production process to be as quick and foolproof as possible. The solution was Lotus's patented Vacuum Assisted Resin Injection (VARI) process. This took some of the best elements of the then state-of-the-art processes, and was designed to avoid the cost of the presses and ovens, but to provide a clean, low-waste moulding process that could produce consistently high-quality mouldings.

The process utilized a pair of matching male and female moulds, made from glass fibre, which would be used to produce a single moulding. Each mould would have a gel coat painted on the inside. Once this had cured, the precut and shaped glass fibre; the body-strengthening 'beams' made from urethane foam; and the cast-alloy bobbins used as fixing points would be laid in the female mould. The second – male – mould was then placed on top of the first mould and the two moulds were fixed together with a rubber seal. The air in the cavity between the two moulds was pumped out and resin (premixed with catalyst) was injected in between the mould in carefully controlled amounts at points all around and in the middle of the mould. The vacuum would 'pull' the resin into the mould, where it would fill the gap between the two moulds, effectively using air pressure instead of an external press, and would soak into the glass fibre. The catalyst would cure the resin at room temperature.

Once the resin was cured the two moulds were separated by pumping compressed air into the moulds and the complete moulding could then be released. As the two halves of the mould had been gel coated, there would be a smooth finish on both sides of the moulding, giving a high-quality finish and no exposed matt. In the Elite's case the body

BODY MOUNTING POINTS

The body bolted to the chassis at fourteen points. Each body mounting point had an oval light-alloy, die-cast bobbin bonded into place which either accepted a through bolt or was threaded to have a bolt screwed into it. The body mounting points were spread symmetrically in pairs along the chassis, the first pair at the very front of the chassis; the second on the front suspension towers; the third at the end of the chassis' front V-section; the fourth and fifth towards the rear of the passenger cell; the sixth on the rear suspension towers; and the seventh and final pair at the rear of the chassis.

was designed to be moulded in two parts, one for the top of the car and one for the bottom, which were joined together by cold gluing. By moulding the body in two halves, top and bottom, the tumble-home on the lower edges of the car could be easily accommodated, as the widest part of the car was the waistline. The join was then covered with a plastic rubbing strip to finish it off neatly.

The use of various kinds of glass-fibre mat and woven cloth could be rigorously controlled in the process, with the appropriate type of glass

All the bodyshells of the Elite family were moulded in two halves – top and bottom. Here an Elite top shell is being removed from its mould. GROUP LOTUS PLC

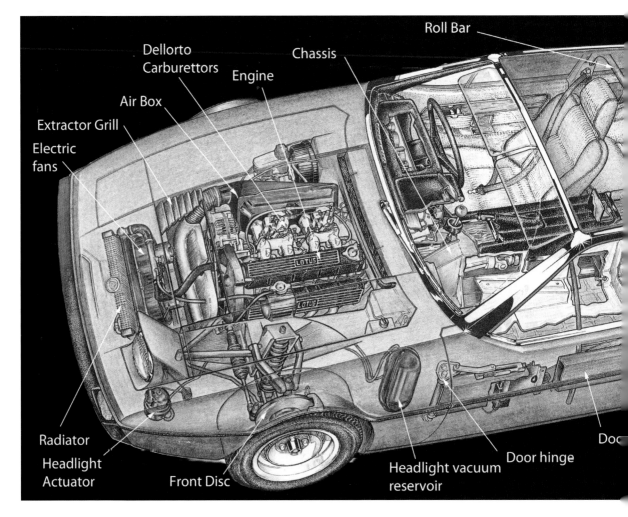

The cutaway of the Elite shows the architecture of the car. GROUP LOTUS PLC

fibre applied in the right position in the mould. In very high stress areas such as the A-pillars Kevlar cloth was used. The use of preformed urethane foam beams in the sills, middle floor box sections, lower A- and B-pillars and in the front bulkhead and scuttle had several functions: they allowed the formation of strong box sections within the body itself using the VARI process; they added significant soundproofing by filling the box sections and cutting down resonances; they enhanced the rigidity of the body's box sections; and they provided additional crash protection to the body's passenger cell. The use of the beams is an excellent example of Chapman's philosophy of making things do more than one job.

Once the top and bottom mouldings were glued together to form a complete shell there was minimal work needed to finish the shell off ready for the assembly line. The smooth finish on both sides of the moulding also assisted production as it was much easier to mount ancillaries accurately (for example in the engine bay) on the precision surface rather than the rough exposed matt as seen on the earlier Elans.

Additional Moulding

Despite being experts in the use and application of glass fibre, Lotus was not blind to new composite and plastics technology. A number of non-

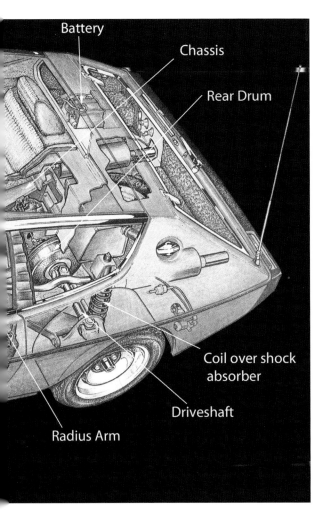

Battery

Chassis

Rear Drum

Coil over shock absorber

Driveshaft

Radius Arm

structural components on the Elite, including the bonnet louvres and the door B-post covers, were vacuum formed in black ABS (Acryonitrile Butadiene Styrene), a type of plastic that was just coming into use at the time and is still in common use for automotive components today. ABS was (and is) relatively strong, tough, impact resistant and easy to mould. After moulding, it had a shiny, impervious surface which, in black, needed no further finishing.

Doors – Part of the 'Ring of Steel'

Safety featured strongly in the body design, as evidenced by the award of the Don Safety Trophy to the car. The car was designed from the start to meet all current and projected safety standards from Europe and the United States, including crash protection from impacts from the front, rear and sides, as well as rollover protection. Side protection was provided by the door beams, while rollover protection was improved by bolting in a 2in (51mm) diameter tubular steel roll bar, which also acted as a roof stiffener and as a locator for the door catches on the B-pillar.

Two widely spaced door hinge brackets were used to mount the door on the A-post. Each bracket was held in place by two bolts which passed through bobbins in the box section that formed the A-post and were bolted to a steel strengthening plate on the inside edge of the A-pillar to fix them firmly in place.

The Elite's doors illustrate Chapman's obsession with making things do more than one job. The Elite had to meet legislation on side-impact protection. So with the bodyshell reinforced with a steel roll bar running in the B-post, which carried the mount for the door latch and a steel hinge mount in the A-post, the door-impact protection was formed using a rectangular steel beam within the door which ran from the hinge on the A-panel to the latch on the B-panel. This beam not only provided the crash resistance, it also carried the lock mechanism, the door catch, the hinge, the electric window motor, glass, glass frame and window operating mechanism. When the door was closed, the beam also provided additional body bracing to help with the body rigidity and improve the passenger cell's resistance to deformation as a result of front- or rear-end shunts. The beam was in effect a one-piece unit, which was then 'wrapped' by the glass-fibre door shell, which was unstressed so that it could be made lighter as its main function was to keep the weather out! The combination of the door beams and the bonded-in roll bar were described by Lotus as the 'Ring of Steel' inside which the passengers were protected from any outside events.

Door Handles

Door handles were flush-fitting units from the British Leyland parts bin (the design was used on the Morris Marina among other cars), as was the flush-fitting internal door catch which, as well as being from a Marina, was the same as that used on the later Elan Plus 2. Despite being a good, reli-

The doors on the Elite were long to give rear-seat passengers relatively easy access.

The Morris Marina external door handles had to be mounted on plinths on the doors to get the right operating angle.

able and trouble-free design, the external handles were probably an unfortunate choice as they were immediately recognizable as coming from a less than premium brand and gave a poor first impression. The handles' prominence was exaggerated by the need to mount them on a protruding plinth moulded into the door skin in order to get them at the right angle.

Door Glass

At the front of the door the glass line rose up to meet with the corner of the windscreen, allowing the glass area to be lower than the base of the screen thereby giving a greater glass area and contributing to the light and airy feeling of the cabin. The whole of the side glass was framed by polished metal extrusions that matched the polished trim on the windscreen and tailgate, and made for a neat and tidy installation.

BONDED GLASS

The glass used in the Elite was special. While many cars at the time still used toughened glass in rubber trim, the Elite's windscreen was bonded in position using Glaverbel VHR 5254 glass, a thin but very high strength laminated glass produced in Belgium. The bonding of the windscreen to the bodyshell played a role in increasing the body's overall torsional strength. The fixed front quarter-lights and rear windows were 5mm toughened glass and were also bonded in place.

While clear glass was standard, tinted glass throughout was offered as an option. Lotus found that it was easier to meet the US regulations for wiper coverage using a single wiper – a single large wiper was also lighter and simpler than a twin (or triple) wiper set-up.

The Front End

The only other separate panel on the body was the front-hinged bonnet, which included the black ABS air extraction grill to its front and had a steel cross-braced frame. The bonnet was secured in place with a pair of cable-operated catches at its rear end and was held up when open by a single gas strut. Along the sill line, just below the door, a thick stainless steel trim strip ran from the rear of the front wheel arch to the front of the rear wheel arch.

At the front of the body the engine was positioned well back behind the front axle line, and with a combination of the engine's low height (due to its 45-degree slant) and the width of the body a very low bonnet line was achieved. This meant the headlamps had to be of the pop-up variety – but that was a Lotus trademark by then, having been used on the Elan and Plus 2, so it was no real hardship.

Airflow Management System

The long flat top of the bonnet incorporated a black ABS vent panel ahead of the actual front-opening bonnet, and this was the visible incarnation of a sophisticated airflow management system that was used to cool the engine, transmission and engine bay and to reduce heat build-up in the car's interior. Air was drawn in at the front of the car through a vent under the front bumper, with two-thirds of it being ducted to pass into the engine radiator and oil cooler and the hot air then extracted through the vent in front of the bonnet. The extracted hot air then flowed over the bonnet and windscreen helping to keep the boundary layer air in place and decreasing drag. The engine bay was isolated from the radiator and its associated duct by a bulkhead in front of the engine.

The remaining third of the incoming air was directed into the engine bay, along each side of the finned engine sump, past the gearbox and along the chassis, exiting around the rear differential, thus providing ambient temperature airflow to help to keep the transmission cool and prevent excessive temperatures in the cabin. The bonnet vents were designed to create a low-pressure area to assist with the flow of cooling air while the car was moving, and the expelled air also provided significant down thrust at the front of the car when it was moving.

The car was equipped with one 11in (279mm) diameter electric fan which was thermostatically operated when needed – usually when the car was in traffic and the airflow needed assistance. The actual radiator was a resin-bonded, all-aluminium unit, the first fitted to a production road car. Cars equipped with air conditioning had twin fans. The ducting moulded into the body also assisted with making the front of the car strong enough to meet crash regulations. The front spoiler positioned under the bumper, as well as providing aerodynamic effect on the whole car, was an important element in the air intake end of the system and was also designed to actively direct cooling air onto the brakes (so should not be removed).

The Rear End

At the rear of the body, the passenger compartment was separated from the boot by a structural bulkhead which was bonded into the bodyshell and included a glass window placed behind the rear seats. This was a slightly strange arrangement

**The black ABS cooling grill enabled hot air from the radiator to be extracted
from the car rather than going into the engine bay.**

The rear hatch, although relatively small, dominated the rear of the Elite.

The swept up rear window and relatively heavy flanks gave a unique style to the Elite.

as it negated some of the advantages of having a rear hatch, in that it prevented the carriage of long loads, but it did add to the rigidity of the bodyshell, cut down on road noise and provide total separation between the fuel tank and the passenger cell.

Directly behind the rear seats, and below the glass divider, was the 14¾gal (67ltr) fuel tank. This was positioned as far forward as possible to be safe in the event of a rear-end shunt, and was fed from two external fuel fillers on the rear C-panel.

The boot, or rear compartment, was a useful 9.7cu ft (275ltr) in size, although it was a bit shallow and rear access was through an all-glass hatchback with a chrome surround which was held in the open position by a pair of gas struts. *Road and Track* identified the volume as only 6.8cu ft (193ltr) – their

measurement was of 'usable' boot space, without luggage obstructing the rear view for the driver. The hatch was opened by cable from within the car; there was no external catch. The glass hatch had bright trim around its periphery and sat on a rubber seal. The hatch was slightly recessed into the body opening, resulting in a small aerodynamic lip at the top and bottom which was designed to avoid the need for separate 'bolt-on' spoilers. This meant the lower run of the hatch opening collected water, so a pair of drain tubes were needed, one at each side, to allow rainwater to drain out of the channel.

The rear-wiper motor was mounted on the rear lower part of the boot lip and the wiper blade automatically parked on the body, so the wiper did not need to be moved to open the hatch. This arrange-

ELITE BODY AERODYNAMICS

The Elite underwent extensive aerodynamic testing during the design process and this resulted in a claimed coefficient of drag (CD) of 0.30 when the car was introduced. This was a considerable achievement by the standards of the time – on its introduction of the C3 Audi 100 in 1982, some eight years later, the VW-Audi group would make much advertising capital of the fact that it too had a CD of 0.30.

The front spoiler was particularly important in this respect, giving both a low drag factor and cutting down on lift, while directing air into the front ducting to cool the engine via the radiator and the gearbox and differential through the ducting. In the original press release for the Elite, Lotus presented the figures obtained from testing the Elite at the MIRA on 9 February 1973 (see table below).

As can be seen from the results, the front spoiler plays a significant part in keeping the front end of the car on the ground as well as improving the coefficient of drag by over 10 per cent. The performance of the car is also improved, the car with the spoiler requiring just 41bhp to drive at 100mph (161km/h) and the car without needing another 4bhp.

In addition to the aerodynamic figures, Tony Rudd was quoted at the time as saying that the airflow when managed by the front spoiler 'reduced engine oil temperature by 8°C, gearbox temperature by 10°C and differential temperature by 16°C' – all significant reductions for the three elements of the drivetrain. The figures are a compelling justification for making sure that the spoiler is always fixed to the Elite.

MIRA Aerodynamic Testing Results on the Lotus Elite, 9 February 1973

		Power needed to reach 100mph (161km/h)	Actual lift at 100mph (161km/h)
With Spoiler Fitted			
Drag Coefficient (CD)	0.30	41bhp	n/a
Coefficient of Lift – Front (CLF)	0.07	n/a	36lb (16.3kg)
Coefficient of Lift – Rear (CLF)	0.08	n/a	41lb (18.6kg)
Without Spoiler Fitted			
Drag Coefficient (CD)	0.33	45bhp	n/a
Coefficient of Lift – Front (CLF)	0.15	n/a	77lb (35kg)
Coefficient of Lift – Rear (CLF)	0.06	n/a	31lb (14.1kg)

ment was revised on the Series 2.2 when the wiper was mounted on the top of the actual hatch, with the wiper hinged at the top and remaining in contact with the glass for its whole run.

The battery and the water bag for the rear screen wash lived in the right-hand corner of the boot, while the fuel pump was on the left-hand side. The full-size spare wheel was slung underneath the luggage area in a wire cradle exposed to road dirt and spray. While this appeared to make the wheel accessible without having to unload the boot, the cradle was secured by a screw that was accessible from the floor of the boot. So if you had a puncture when touring, you would unfortunately still have to unload some of the contents of the boot to access the spare.

Aerodynamics

During the development of the Elite many hours were spent in the wind tunnel at the Motor Industry Research Association (MIRA), to refine the car's overall body coefficient of drag to make it as low as possible as well as to enhance the car's stability, especially in crosswinds, and to tweak the aerodynamic features that supported the operation of other parts of the car, such as the engine cooling system, the rear spoilers and the transmission and rear differential cooling. As such the body played an important role in the overall efficiency of the car – particularly important in the light of the fuel crisis and ever-increasing price of petrol in the 1970s.

The body was painted using ICI P-407 two-pack polyurethane paint. This paint needed a separate catalyst for hardening, and Lotus recommended respraying a complete panel if paint repairs were needed, as, unlike cellulose, the paint would not 'reflow' the original paint if a patch was attempted.

INTERIOR

The Elite's interior was designed by Italian stylist Giorgetto Giugiaro at his design house Italdesign. Chapman, realizing that the market he was aiming at would not tolerate a 'thrown together' kit-car interior, wanted a design that was both integrated and attractive, and which would stand comparison with the other cars, both low and high volume models, in the four-seat GT market.

Seating

The prime function of the interior was to seat four adults in comfort within the constraints of the overall design – the main limiting factors being the height of the roof, the body's 'cross-member' boxes, and the high and wide transmission tunnel needed to clear the chassis. While this presented few problems in the front, the rear seats were more of a challenge. The solution was to move away from the traditional bench seat and design a pair of carefully sculpted seats tailored to the car's body. This resulted in a high bolster under the thighs, a deep seating area and a semi-reclined (but fixed) backrest, all of which were built into the body and upholstered – there were no separate seat frames as such. The seats were actually reasonably comfortable and incorporated built-in headrests, which added to the car's passive safety but detracted from its active safety as they tended to obstruct the rear view – contemporary road tests asked if they couldn't have been made removable.

There was an open storage compartment on the outside edge of each rear seat. The pull-out opener for the rear hatch was located in the offside one. The rear and front seats were separated by a wide shelf over the transmission tunnel, which wrapped around the gear and handbrake levers and incorporated a shallow storage tray. The rest of the cabin was fully trimmed – the headlining was cloth and the instrument binnacle and dashboard top was trimmed in a flock-type material called Marcasite.

At the front there was a pair of adjustable seats which could slide forwards and back on runners and had adjustable backrests along with built-in fixed headrests. Each seat incorporated a clever hinge-and-move mechanism that allowed the seat to move forward and the backrest to hinge forward to allow full access to the rear seats. Operation of the mechanism did not affect the seats' original settings so the seat position remained the same when the seat was reset. The rear seats had fittings for inertia-reel safety belts, while both of the front seats had three-point inertia-reel safety belts.

The rear seats were heavily sculptured to accommodate two people. A window separated the passenger compartment from the luggage bay.

The S1 Elite interior used a flocked nylon material on the dash. This car has the optional leather-covered seats.

The Elite's dashboard was shared with the Eclat, and was comprehensively equipped with instruments. GROUP LOTUS PLC

Other Interior Features

Dashboard
In front of the driver there was a neat integrated dashboard mounted in a binnacle which presented the driver with a comprehensive set of circular instruments, all made by Smiths and having black faces and bevels and white lettering and needles. These comprised speedometer and rev counter, both 4in in diameter, flanked by four smaller instruments gauging fuel, water temperature, oil pressure and battery voltage. To the outside of the smaller instruments were rectangular warning lights, four on each side.

A secondary panel sat over the instrument panel to integrate the unit and lose the bitty appearance that the separate instruments could engender. On the passenger side there was a lockable glovebox.

Steering Wheel and Handbrake
The steering wheel was a two-spoke affair with a large, soft, rectangular crash pad fixed across its width to protect the driver in a crash. The handbrake was – at last for a Lotus – fixed in the conventional position on the centre console (after a decade of the Elans using an umbrella-type puller under the dashboard) and a coin tray was positioned in front of the lever. Ashtrays for front and rear passengers were also on the centre console, and rear passengers had a shallow tray let into the console.

Trim
A choice of velour or leather upholstery could be specified. The dashboard binnacle, along with the dash top and sides of the centre console, were trimmed in Marcasite, a cropped nylon trim material that had a slightly furry effect, probably best described as a 1970s attempt to mimic suede.

Centre Console
The centre console housed six Triumph-sourced rocker switches to operate the electric windows, rear wash and wipe, hazard flashers and rear screen heater, along with a pair of pull switches for the main lights and panel light, a pair of air vents, the

The Series 2 Elite's interior was well trimmed and an attractive place to be in. In front of the passenger was a large glove locker.

One quirk with the Elite was the tiny spotlight used to illuminate the switches on the centre console. Positioned next to the interior light on the roll-bar casing, it was a good idea but sometimes didn't work in practice.

radio (or radio cassette player), clock, heater or air-conditioning controls, cigar lighter and heater fan control. The faces of the console and glove-box, plus the coin trays in the centre console, were covered in a thin wood veneer that contrived to look like plastic and is now considered to be the epitome of 1970s kitsch.

ELITE SPECIFICATION OPTIONS

The Elite was a well-equipped car as standard, and its basic specification included:

- Heater
- Radio
- Five-speed gearbox
- Alloy wheels
- Quartz halogen headlights
- Door mirrors
- Electric windows
- Heated rear window
- Rear screen wipe and wash
- Inertia-reel front seat belts
- Front and rear head restraints
- Rear seat-belt mountings
- Hazard warning lights
- 4.1:1 rear differential
- Tinted glass
- Automatic aerial extension
- Marcasite/cropped nylon trim

This standard equipment was supplied in the Elite 501. Lotus offered three more levels of options to the buyers, each one a step up from the last.

502 options:

- Air conditioning
- Stereo radio tape deck

503 options:

- Air conditioning
- Stereo radio tape deck
- Power steering

504 options:

- Air conditioning
- Stereo radio tape deck
- Power steering
- Automatic gearbox
- 3.73:1 rear differential

The switches and controls mounted on the centre console had to be illuminated to meet US safety legislation. Rather than fitting a simple light above or below the console, or fitting individual lighting to each control like most manufacturers did, Lotus – as usual – took a different route. The courtesy light mounted on the centre of the cockpit roof incorporated a tiny spotlight trained on the console to provide the required light. It was an ingenious solution that worked well but was prone to problems (one contemporary road test had the light flickering on and off, much to the annoyance of the driver) and relied on perfect alignment of the projector unit for the light to hit the right spot.

Ventilation

The ventilation system was carefully designed to ensure adequate through flow of air in the cabin and the extraction of 'used' air. The main extraction points for old air were on the B-posts, and the ABS mouldings on the outside of the body were designed to provide low-pressure areas to suck air out of the interior and there were secondary extractors in the C-post.

Air conditioning, when fitted, comprised a 340sq in condenser in front of the radiator and a second electric fan to operate the cooling. An engine-driven Frigidaire axial compressor unit was mated to a receiver/dryer unit which fitted on the front bulkhead in the place of the standard heater unit. The interior fan had three settings, and two sliders controlled the heat setting and direction of airflow. The through flow of air was controlled through extractor outlets on the B- and C-posts. If air conditioning was not fitted, the standard fitment comprised an inlet air unit with heater matrix, and three-speed blower with air-direction control.

ELECTRICAL SYSTEM

As a luxury car, the Elite had a high level of equipment, much of it electrically powered. The electrical system was carefully designed to overcome the problems inherent with a glass-fibre car – the main one being its complexity as it needed to provide separate earth (or return) connections to every component mounted on the bodyshell.

The Elite's wiring loom used the British Standard BS6862 for wire colours, keeping it in line with the rest of the motor industry. The loom was split into three main sections – the engine bay, fascia and rear. It was designed with the minimum number of connections and had a single route from the interior to the engine bay via a hole in the double-skinned wheel arch. The loom passed through the hole and was protected by a rubber grommet.

The instrument panel in the fascia was designed to carry all the switches for the various functions, and also included wiring for the standard Philips type 312 radio and the optional Philips type 712 radio cassette with microphone option. Speakers for the radio were mounted in the rear luggage bins on the outer edge of the rear seats. The steering column stalks were British Leyland type, with the left-hand stalk operating the windscreen wipers and washers and the right-hand stalk operating the headlamp flash and dip, horn, and turn indicators. Warning lights for handbrake on or brake fail, hazard warning lights, main beam, rear screen heater, left and right direction indicators, low fuel, ignition on and seat belt warning were fitted in the instrument console in front of the driver, four on each side of the main instrument cluster. While the instrument panel looked the part and gave plenty of information to the driver, the instrument glass could be troubled by reflections.

The front lights were Lucas 7in-diameter 75/50W sealed beam units (with 60/55W halogen units as an option) mounted in the pop-up pods, with a combined side and indicator unit in the front bumper. In true Lotus tradition the Elite's pop-up headlamps were vacuum operated, using a rust-prone vacuum tank positioned in the left-hand side of the bulkhead, which was mounted on the door hinge reinforcing plate. A single pipe from the manifold and a pair of pipes to each headlamp's vacuum cylinder were fitted to an adaptor on the tank. A non-return valve was fitted between the manifold and the vacuum tank to maintain the vacuum (and hence keep the headlamps down) when the engine was turned off. The system was fail-safe as the lights were spring-loaded and were designed to stay up if there was a vacuum failure.

With both headlights up the wedge shape is compromised but the car still looks good.

The system did result in the lights raising themselves slowly over time when the engine was off – or quicker if there was a dodgy non-return valve or leak in the system. The author's father's Eclat displayed just such behaviour, especially when left in the pub car park, when the car would appear to be winking to the crowd as one headlamp slowly raised itself soon after the car was parked.

The rectangular rear light cluster – combining the stop, tail, indicator, reflector and reverse lights – was shared with the Aston Martin V8 'Oscar India' models. Each cluster was fitted in a recessed opening on the outer edge of the rear bumper where they were protected from minor parking shunts. The rear number plate was fitted in a deep recess between the two light clusters

If there is a vacuum leak on a Series 1 car, one or other of the headlamps will slowly rise when the engine is off, making it look like the car is winking.

Series 1 cars had small light clusters, shared with the Aston Martin V8. Note also that on Series 1 cars the rear wiper was mounted at the bottom of the rear screen.

and was illuminated by a pair of small lights fitted in the outside edges of the bumper recess.

The interior had two single lights sited on the roll bar for the front-seat passengers, a single light on the rear bulkhead for rear-seat passengers, a glovebox light, and a spotlight mounted on the roll bar to illuminate the central instrument panel. Additional lights were fitted to the door-open reflectors, in the boot and in the bonnet to illuminate the engine when the bonnet was open.

The electrical system was fed by an engine-mounted 45A alternator (a 60A version was fitted to cars with air conditioning) which was powered by a V-belt shared with the water pump. The battery was a 50Ah unit positioned in the boot.

THE ORIGINAL ELITE

The original Lotus Type 14 Elite was a two-door coupé aimed at both road and racing use and was introduced in 1957 and produced until 1963, although limited numbers of the cars built up from spare bodyshells were sold through to the mid-1960s. Colin Chapman and the Elite's stylist Peter Kirwan-Taylor identified a number of design criteria for the Elite:

• it should be suitable for road and rally use
• it should be capable of winning its class at the Le Mans 24 Hours race
• it should use an all-glass-fibre monocoque
• its suspension was to be based on the Formula 2 Lotus 12

• the engine would be the new all-alloy Coventry Climax FWE engine
• the cabin would accommodate two average-sized adults – with Chapman himself acting as the model.

Fully equipped as a road-legal car, the Elite was virtually unique at the time as it used GRP for the entire bodyshell, which was a monocoque design with no separate chassis, albeit with some steel reinforcing plates bonded in at strategic locations. The Elite was light and rigid, had a great performance and handled superbly and was judged to be a very successful competition car. As a measure of its success as a competition car, the

Elite won its class at the Le Mans 24 Hours race every year from 1959 to 1963. However, despite its success at Le Mans, the major road race of the time, the Elite's credentials as a road car, especially a grand tourer, were undermined by its relative lack of sophistication – most notably, road tests of the day found it to be noisy and hence tiring to use over long distances.

After production ceased, Chapman acknowledged that the Elite was in fact 60 per cent racer and 40 per cent road car, and that – probably more important than its lack of refinement – it was very expensive to make. The Elite's high cost was largely due to Lotus's lack of production capacity at the

time. This meant that body production had to be outsourced, first to boat builder Maximar then to the Bristol Aircraft Factory, and the engine had to be bought in from Coventry Climax. Named the FWE (Feather Weight Elite), this 4-cylinder engine was over square with a bore and stroke of 76.2 x 66.7mm and sported an all-alloy head and crankcase with a single overhead camshaft. The complete engine weighed a mere 215lb (97.5kg), justifying its name and assisting Chapman in his pursuit of lightness. The engine produced 72bhp in its initial single SU carburetted form, and later produced a healthy 83bhp when fitted with twin SU carburettors. It also had reasonable torque of 77lb ft at 3,800rpm, and was easy to tune if required. The only problem with the engine was that it was virtually a hand-built racing unit and was not cheap.

The original Elite was officially in production from 1958 through to 1963, and around 1,000 cars were produced. As the cars were complex to build and the monocoque body and the Coventry Climax engine were both expensive to buy in the price charged for the car had to be high, and this obviously limited the car's appeal. One of the major lessons learned from the original Elite was that costs could be controlled by bringing production in-house, a lesson carried forwards with the Elan and personified with the new Elite, where virtually every major component was Lotus made.

The original Elite was a beautiful car and won its class at Le Mans 24 Hours several years in a row.

ELITE AND ECLAT SERIES 2.2

The Lotus Type 83 Elite Series 2.2 and the Lotus Type 84 Eclat Series 2.2 were introduced in 1980. The major mechanical changes included the adoption of the 912 2.2-litre engine in favour of the 907 unit; a five-speed Getrag manual gearbox to replace the Lotus item; and a fully galvanized chassis. There were also a host of minor improvements. Externally the cars were badged 'Series 2.2' to reflect the increased engine capacity, and the Lotus standard options (501 to 504) were dropped, to be replaced with a list of optional extras that could be specified by the customer when the car was ordered.

Exterior

While the base bodyshell mouldings were unchanged, the Elite Series 2.2's appearance was changed subtly by the addition of a new front spoiler, sill extensions and a new rear bumper. The front spoiler was more angular than the Series 1 unit and was extended around the sides of the car to the front wheel arches. There was a wide oblong air intake in the front and the whole spoiler was body coloured. The sill covers sat below the doors and like the front spoiler were also body coloured (unlike the black S1 sills). The chrome strip below the doors that had been a feature on the S1 was discarded.

At the rear, a new bumper carried large integrated rear light clusters, sourced from the Rover SD1, and had a recess for a square number plate – necessitating a two-line plate, as usually seen on motorbikes, for the UK cars. The rear light cluster incorporated a high-intensity fog light as required by current legislation. The rear of the Elite Series 2.2 was further cleaned up by repositioning the rear wiper at the top of the rear window and having a separate catch to open the tailgate positioned on the rear panel. The rear wiper motor was mounted

The Series 2 Elite and Eclat had a number of significant mechanical improvements, but the styling was only tweaked.
GROUP LOTUS PLC

The Series 2 rear wiper was moved to the top of the screen, with a clever mechanism to drive the wiper from the roof-mounted motor.

on the roof of the luggage area, and a clever cam mechanism was used to allow the drive to the wiper to be disconnected when the window was opened.

Interior

The interior of the cars was upgraded slightly, with a new layout for the instruments in the binnacle in front of the driver, a revised centre console and repositioned electric window switches. The instrument console retained the two large dials (speedometer and rev counter) and the four smaller instruments (fuel level, oil pressure, engine temperature and battery voltage) but the oil pressure and water temperature instruments sat between the speedometer and rev counter, while the fuel gauge was to the left of the cluster and the voltmeter was to the right.

Underneath each set of the outer instruments were two strips of four warning lights which were blacked out when not illuminated. As in the Series I cars a separate panel covered the instrument panel and could be upholstered to match the dashboard.

Contrasting views of the Series 1 (right) and Series 2 Elite (left) show the latter's new rear bumper and Rover SD1 tail lights, as well as the repositioned wiper.

The Series 2 interior was slightly more luxurious than the S1, with leather trim a common and popular option.

The centre console was simplified to carry new British Leyland-sourced toggle switches and was split into five layers. From the top, left to right, there were two toggle switches for the rear washer and wiper; an analogue or, on later cars, a red LED digital clock; and two toggle switches for the lights and fog lights. Below this was a panel with three rotary switches to control the heating and ventilation, and below that a cigar lighter, two more toggle switches for the heated rear window and hazard warning lights, and an instrument light dimmer. Below this row was a pair of ventilation outlets and below them the radio cassette player.

The lighting of the centre console switches was changed from the spotlight system used on Series 1 cars to one that used fibre-optic cables to transfer light from a central source to the symbols on the switches. Unfortunately, as with the original spotlight system, owners found it wasn't very effective. The light switch did have a permanently illuminated light on it to enable the driver to find it in a dark car.

Declining Sales

In general, the Series 2.2 Elite and Eclat with their galvanized chassis, torquier 2.2-litre engine and Getrag gearbox offered significant mechanical improvements over the original cars and their lightly revised and updated interiors made them even more civilized. The main problem with the Elite (and Eclat) 2.2 was the price. When the cars were launched the base model Elite 2.2 was £16,433, but prices rose steeply and by late 1981 customers were being asked to pay £17,206 for the Elite 2.2 and £16,751 for the Eclat. In October 1981 Lotus slashed £1,894 off the price of the base model Eclat 2.2, following suit in January 1982 with a £1,616 reduction in the price of the Elite. While this did stimulate sales of the Eclat, sales of the Elite remained disappointing and by the end of 1982 Elite production was stopped.

Elite and Eclat Riviera

A 'Riviera' special edition of the Elite and Eclat Series 2.2 was launched in the early 1980s to boost sales. The only change to the standard car was the addition of a large lift-out glass sunroof. The removable glass panel over the front seats ran across the full width of the roof, creating a panoramic effect for the passengers. As a £404.84 option the sunroof was not cheap but it did tempt some buyers.

A late 'special edition' of the Elite and Eclat was the 1982 Riviera, with a lift-out, panoramic glass sunroof. GROUP LOTUS PLC

From the rear the Riviera glass roof can be discerned on this Elite.

LOTUS ELITE (1974–80) AND ELITE S2.2 (1980–82) SPECIFICATIONS

Layout and chassis   Two-door, four-seat sports coupé with glass-reinforced plastic body and separate steel
chassis and rear-wheel drive

Engine
Type   Lotus 45-degree slant-4
Block material   Die-cast light alloy
Head material   Die-cast light alloy
Cylinders   4 in line
Cooling   Water/antifreeze mix
Bore and stroke   95.2 x 69.2mm (S2.2 95.29 x 76.2mm)
Capacity   1973cc (S2.2 2172cc)
Valves   4 valves per cylinder, operated by belt-driven dohc
Compression ratio   9.5:1 (S2.2 9.44:1)
Carburettor   UK and Europe: twin Dellorto twin choke DHLA 45E
                          USA: twin Zenith Stromberg 175 CD-2SE constant velocity
Max. power (claimed)   UK and Europe: 160bhp at 6,500rpm
                          USA: 140bhp at 6,600rpm
                          S2.2 160bhp at 6,500rpm
Max. torque   UK and Europe: 140lb ft at 5,000rpm
                          USA: 130lb ft at 5,000rpm
                          S2.2 160lb ft at 5,000rpm
Fuel capacity   14.75gal (67ltr)

Transmission
Gearbox (manual)   Lotus five-speed all synchromesh (S2.2 Getrag five-speed all synchromesh)
Clutch   Single dry plate
Ratios   1st   3.20:1 (S2.2 2.96:1)
            2nd   2.01:1 (S2.2 1.93:1)
            3rd   1.37:1 (S2.2 1.39:1)
            4th   1.00:1 (S2.2 1.00:1)
            5th   0.80:1 (S2.2 0.813:1)
            Reverse   3.467:1 (S2.2 3.71:1)
Gearbox (automatic)   Borg Warner three-speed BW65 with manual override on 1st and 2nd gears
Ratios   1st   2.39:1
            2nd   1.45:1
            3rd   1.0:1
            Reverse   2.09:1
            Final drive   3.73:1 (S2.2 4.1:1)

Suspension and Steering

Front	Independent by upper twin wishbones, single lower link, anti-roll bar, coil springs over telescopic dampers
Rear	Independent by radius arm, lateral link, coil springs over telescopic dampers
Steering	Rack-and-pinion (power-operated option)
Tyres	205/60 VR x 14 radial
Wheels	7JK x 14in-diameter cast aluminium alloy
Rim width	7in (Sprint 6in)

Brakes

Type	Front discs and rear drums with servo assistance
Size	10.44in front, 9 x 2.25in rear

Dimensions

Track

Front	58.5in (1,486mm)
Rear	59in (1,499mm)
Wheelbase	97.8in (2,484mm)
Overall length	175.5in (4,458mm)
Overall width	71.5in (1,816mm)
Overall height	47.5in (1,207mm)

Unladen weight

Basic kerb:	2,450lb (1,111kg) (S2.2 2,469lb/1,120kg)

Performance

Top speed	125mph (201km/h) (S2.2 127mph/204km/h)
0–60mph	8.1sec (S2.2: 7.5sec)

CHAPTER THREE

THE ECLAT – PRODUCTION AND DEVELOPMENTS

ECLAT

Introduced to the public on 15 October 1975 after the Elite had been in production for a year, the Lotus Type 83 Eclat was initially marketed as a replacement for the Elan Plus 2. Described as the 'Eclat 2+2 or occasional four-seat sports car' in contemporary Lotus literature, the Eclat was a coupé with a sporting pedigree which undercut the price of the Elite by a significant amount (just under 10 per cent), giving Lotus a new lead-in model to the range.

The range mirrored that of the Elite, but with four equipment option levels (520 to 523) at launch. The 521, 522 and 523 option packs were equivalent to the Elite's 501, 502 and 503 packs. The base model Eclat, the 520, was introduced at the same time as a 'poverty spec' version designed with minimum equipment to keep the headline price of the range down. The base model Eclat 520 was equipped with 5½J x 13-in steel wheels with 185/70 x 13 radial tyres; an exhaust system with a single pipe; a four-speed gearbox from the then current Granada; and a higher rear-axle ratio

The Eclat was essentially a coupé version of the Elite. The base model Eclat (the 520) shown here had steel wheels and a four-speed gearbox to keep costs down. GROUP LOTUS PLC

This shot of the base model Eclat shows the single fuel filler on the left-hand side. GROUP LOTUS PLC

(3.73:1) to make up for the lack of a fifth gear. As a cost saving exercise the reduced specification was a success, allowing the Eclat 520 to be priced at launch in the UK at £5,729, significantly cheaper than the Elite 501's £6,483.

In early 1976 the Eclat 524 was launched with the Borg Warner automatic gearbox as used on the Elite 504. During the life of the Elite and the Eclat, the Eclat was priced around 9.5 per cent cheaper than the Elite – as exemplified by Lotus's official UK prices for September 1978, reproduced below:

Elite		Eclat	
n/a	n/a	520	£10,231.66
501	£11,503.45	521	£10,989.82
502	£12,517.84	522	£11,991.34
503	£12,989.34	523	£12,428.92
504	£13,149.64	524	£12,590.38

Mechanically the Eclat was in the main identical to the equivalent Elite with the exception of the base model Eclat 520. While the moulding of the lower body half was the same as the Elite, the major change was in the upper body moulding, although this was identical to the Elite's apart from the rear end to accommo-

date the sloping coupé tail and lidded luggage compartment.

The rear end featured a sloping fixed rear window which carried its line onto a large boot lid, giving 'fastback' coupé styling that resulted in a much more conventional appearance than the Elite. Visibility was also improved over the Elite as the rear side windows extended further back than the Elite's, and the bottom of the rear side window line remained straight rather than sweeping up as in the Elite. The increased glass area gave a better rear three-quarter view for the driver. The coupé styling meant that headroom for the rear passengers was compromised but apart from this the passenger cell remained the same size as that on the Elite, giving relatively good legroom front and rear; and the Eclat's rear passengers were still better provided for than in many competing coupés.

The Elite's rear built-in headrests were not present in the Eclat, but rear visibility (for example when parking) was still poor as the lower edge of the rear window was still relatively high. The Eclat lost the Elite's rear windscreen washer, and the separate 13cu ft (368ltr) capacity boot was significantly larger than the Elite's.

The Eclat also only had a single fuel filler cap (on the nearside) rather than the Elite's pair. The

All Eclats apart
from the base model
came with alloy
wheels and the Lotus
five-speed gearbox.
GROUP LOTUS PLC

While this Series 2 Eclat has had an engine transplant it shows the simple rear-end styling and the revised rear bumper with Rover tail lights.

This two-tone Eclat shows the neat styling and the S2's revised front spoiler.

Lotus made a lot of the Eclat's boot space. Here an S2 is being loaded up.
GROUP LOTUS PLC

design of the boot lid allowed the rear lip to wrap over the opening and form the top rear face of the rear panel, allowing easy drainage of water from the boot surround without having to resort to the Elite's separate drain tubes.

One adverse impact of the Eclat's restyled body was that the coefficient of drag was raised from the Elite's 0.30 to 0.34. The Eclat was accepted by the press of the day as a cheaper fastback version of the Elite, offering equivalent performance but reduced visibility and rear headroom. As well as retaining all the safety features of the Elite, the Eclat was a more conventional looking car and was popular – sales of the Eclat in the UK and the rest of the world were pretty much level with the Elite from 1977 onwards and the Eclat outsold the Elite significantly between 1976 and 1978, and was only slightly less popular in the last two years of exports (1979–80) to the United States.

ECLAT SPECIFICATION OPTIONS

When it was introduced, the Eclat had a significantly lower specification than the Elite, but for the standards of the time was still a reasonably well-equipped car as standard. In its basic Eclat 520 form, its specification included:

- Heater
- Four-speed gearbox
- Steel wheels with 185/70 HR radial tyres
- Quartz halogen headlights
- Electric windows
- Heated rear window
- Inertia-reel front seat belts
- Front head restraints
- Rear seat-belt mountings
- Hazard warning lights
- 3.73:1 rear differential

As with the Elite, Lotus offered four more levels of options to the Eclat buyers – the 521, 522, 523 and 524 – each one a step up from the last. The Eclat 521 options were broadly in line with the Elite 501 options.

521 options – as per 520, plus:

- Radio
- Five-speed gearbox
- Alloy wheels and 250/60 VR radial tyres
- Door mirrors
- 4.1:1 rear differential
- Tinted glass
- Automatic aerial extension
- Marcasite/cropped nylon trim

522 options – as per 521, plus:

- Air conditioning
- Stereo radio cassette deck

523 options – as per 522, plus:
- Power steering

524 options – as per 523, plus:
- Automatic gearbox
- 3.73:1 rear differential

LOTUS SPRINT – THE US VERSION OF THE ECLAT

Launched in the United States in 1976, the Eclat was initially called simply the Lotus Sprint – presumably to gather some glory from the relatively well-known Elan Sprint and to place the Eclat as a more sporting car than the luxury Elite. While it was identical mechanically to the UK-market Eclat, with the same option packs, the base model Sprint was equipped with a catalyst and air pump to meet the 1976 emissions requirements. The 'Sprint' name was quietly dropped by 1978, with 'Eclat' reinstated, although in a 1978 *Road and Track* magazine test of the Elite and Eclat they pointed out that the Eclat still carried a 'Sprint' decal on the boot.

The final year the Eclat was exported to the United States was 1980, when only approximately twenty were sold. The car was, along with the Elite, killed off in that market by a combination of Lotus's poor financial state and ever-increasing emissions legislation.

The Eclat was originally marketed in the United States as the Lotus 'Sprint'. GROUP LOTUS PLC

The Lotus Sprint was an Eclat in all but name. This press car has aftermarket alloy wheels to lift the 'poverty' specification. GROUP LOTUS PLC

ELITE AND ECLAT IN THE UNITED STATES

At the introduction of the Elite in 1974, Lotus distributed cars in the United States using a network of independent dealers, with no overall marketing or planning functions. Recognizing that this was not ideal, Lotus set up Lotus Cars of America with the intention of having a single organization running the Lotus operation in North America. Financial problems ensued with the new organization and – faced with falling sales during 1978 and 1979 – Lotus stepped in to set up Lotus North America Inc. to try to save the situation. This led to a tie-up with Rolls-Royce in 1979, where Rolls-Royce would sell Lotus cars through its US dealerships. This smart move was however stalled almost immediately as during 1979–80 the US dollar to UK pound exchange rate moved against the pound by over 40 per cent – making the already expensive Lotus even more pricy in the United States.

In January 1975 at its launch in the United States the Elite was priced at $15,460 (West Coast) and $15,500 (East Coast); the Lotus Eclat (or Sprint) launched at $12,900 (East Coast) in November 1976. By 1978 the Elite was some $29,000 and the Eclat followed closely behind at about $28,000, where it competed directly with cars such as Mercedes SL, BMW 633CSi, Jaguar XJ-S and even the Porsche 928. But it got worse – in 1980, the Eclat was listed at $36,100 when a BMW 633CSi was $31,870 and a Porsche 911SC was $27,700.

The US press, while still appreciating the Lotus's handling performance and roadholding, were asking questions about the use of a 4-cylinder engine and the quality and reliability of the cars and were coming to the conclusion that they were just not competitive with the opposition from Europe. Rolls-Royce sales suffered as well with the massive price increases generated by the exchange-rate changes, and the Lotus–Rolls-Royce deal was seen to be dead by the end of 1981, with a public announcement made in 1982.

Lotus set up a new operation in the United States, Lotus Performance Cars LP, to handle sales of the Esprit. However, the Excel was not marketed there. While the car still met US crash regulations, it would have had to have been resubmitted for emissions testing due to the different ratios of the Toyota gearbox – the costs were more than Lotus could afford at the time.

ECLAT SPRINT

Not to be confused with the 'Sprint' marketed in the United States, the Eclat Sprint was launched in the UK in 1977 as a £298.35 factory-fitted option pack available on the Eclat 520 and 521. The option pack was designed to offer a more aggressively styled Eclat to cash in on the performance end of the market. The Sprint option comprised black stripes on the flanks and the bonnet and an all-black boot lid, together with a black interior. An oil cooler was also fitted.

The Sprint badge on the rear panel incorporated a patriotic red, white and blue Union flag as its background, and 'Sprint' was incorporated into the side stripes just behind the front wheel.

The 520-based Sprint was fitted with special 5½J 13in alloy wheels with 185/70 HR 13 tyres and retained the 520's four-speed gearbox and 3.73:1 final drive, while the 521-based Sprints wore the standard 7J x 14in alloys common to the rest of the range and kept the Lotus five-speed box and 4.1:1 final drive.

The Eclat Sprint shown here is the UK special edition with its stripes, logos and minor upgrades.

The Eclat Sprint had 'Sprint' logos on the front as well as the stripe.

The cars for the US market had marker lights on their flanks but were otherwise virtually identical to the UK cars. Mechanically the Federal cars had Stromberg carburettors and a detuned engine to meet emissions legislation. GROUP LOTUS PLC

JOHN WALSH'S 1979 ECLAT 523

John Walsh owns an interesting Eclat which he bought in 2007 – it is a 1979 model, first registered in 1980, and for the first five years of its life it was owned by Lotus. Research by John showed that the car was first registered in the name of the then current Lotus F1 team manager, Andrew Ferguson, and that the car was used as a team run-around for the drivers (Nigel Mansell and Elio De Angelis) as well as a PR car.

The car was delivered in gold metallic paint, Lotus Code A04, which was presumably Lotus Championship Gold, a metallic finish usually seen on the S2.2 cars. With the 523 specification the car had air conditioning and power steering as standard, as well as a luxury ermine-coloured cloth interior. The car remained in Lotus's hands until January 1985 when the car was sold on the open market. It eventually fell into the hands of a new owner, Julian Yell, who did a full body-off rebuild and restoration in 1996–97 when its colour was changed to Lotus Yellow. The car was shown at the Club Lotus Castle Combe track day, where it won best in show.

Having completed the car to a high standard, Julian sold the car to make way for his next restoration. John eventually came across the Eclat on the Pistonheads website and bought it for £1,000 without seeing it. It was abandoned in a garden in Cumbria and needed some mechanical and cosmetic restoration before it could be got back on the road.

The car has been christened 'Banana' as a result of John taking the car to its first show. A little girl and her parents walked past the car with its bright yellow paint and its proud owner, and said 'Ooh, look Mummy, a squashed banana' – possibly not what the owner wanted to hear but the name has stuck. In any case the Lotus Yellow paint makes the car stand out from the crowds and is of course an iconic Lotus colour.

During its time in John's ownership (or rather, as John claims, it has owned him) Banana has had its engine, gearbox and differential rebuilt, along with a complete overhaul of the brakes, but John has been careful to keep the car as standard as possible – it still has the original radio cassette player. The worst job he found was removing the differential – he had broken it going too fast over a humpback bridge and Banana obviously didn't want it changed as she fought John all the way.

Driving the car is one of John's great joys – he loves the handling although he finds that Banana can be a handful on wet roads when the rear end can let go. He is running her on Goodyear NCT Eagles at the moment but as these are getting hard to find he is not sure what to go on to. There are two downsides to the car. The first is the brakes – no matter what he does to them he finds they do not inspire confidence. The second is that it seems to attract more flies than something you'll find in a field of cows and is a nightmare to keep clean.

The car cruises comfortably at motorway speeds and the acceleration is, as John describes it, 'pretty nimble for her age'. The high point of John's relationship with Banana was when it was used as the bride's car for his wedding; apparently his wife is now happy to clean the highly polished alloy wheels and it is a permanent member of the family.

John Walsh's Eclat was his wedding car – here is he and his wife on the happy day. JOHN WALSH

LOTUS ECLAT (1974–80), ECLAT SPRINT/520 AND ECLAT S2.2 (1980–82) SPECIFICATIONS

Layout and chassis　Two door, 2+2 seat sports coupé with glass-reinforced plastic body, conventional rear boot and separate steel chassis and rear-wheel drive.

Engine

Type	Lotus 45-degree slant-4
Block material	Die-cast light alloy
Head material	Die cast light alloy
Cylinders	4 in line
Cooling	Water/antifreeze mix
Bore and stroke	95.2 x 69.2mm (S2.2 95.29 x 76.2mm)
Capacity	1973cc (S2.2 2172cc)
Valves	4 valves per cylinder, operated by belt-driven dohc
Compression ratio	9.5 :1 (S2.2 9.44:1)
Carburettor	UK and Europe: twin Dellorto twin choke DHLA 45E
	USA: twin Zenith Stromberg 175 CD-2SE constant velocity
Max. power (claimed)	
	UK and Europe: 160bhp at 6,500rpm
	USA: 140bhp at 6,600rpm
	S2.2 160bhp at 6,500rpm
Max. torque	UK and Europe: 140lb ft at 5,000rpm
	USA: 130lb ft at 5,000rpm
	S2.2 160lb ft at 5,000rpm
Fuel capacity	14.75gal (67ltr)

Transmission

Gearbox (manual)		Lotus five-speed all synchromesh (Sprint Ford four-speed; S2.2 Getrag five-speed all syncromesh)
Clutch		Single dry plate
Ratios	1st	3.20:1 (Eclat Sprint 3.16:1, S2.2 2.96:1)
	2nd	2.01:1 (Eclat Sprint 1.94:1, S2.2 1.93:1)
	3rd	1.37:1 (Eclat Sprint 1.41:1, S2.2 1.39:1)
	4th	1.00:1 (Eclat Sprint 1.00:1, S2.2 1.00:1)
	5th	0.80:1 (Eclat Sprint n/a, S2.2 0.813:1)
	Reverse	3.467:1 (S2.2 3.71:1)
Gearbox (automatic)		Borg Warner three-speed BW65 with manual override on 1st and 2nd gears
Ratios	1st	2.39:1
	2nd	1.45:1
	3rd	1.0:1
	Reverse	2.09:1
Final drive		3.73:1 (Eclat Sprint 4-speed, S2.2 4.1:1)

Suspension and Steering
Front	Independent by upper twin wishbones, single lower link, anti-roll bar, coil springs over telescopic dampers
Rear	Independent by radius arm, lateral link, coil springs over telescopic dampers
Steering	Rack-and-pinion (power operated option)
Tyres	205/60 VR x 14 radial
Wheels	7JK x14in-diameter cast aluminium alloy
Rim width	7in (Sprint 6in)

Brakes
Type	Front discs and rear drums with servo assistance
Size	10.44in front, 9 x 2.25in rear

Dimensions
Track	
Front	58.5in (1,486mm)
Rear	59in (1,499mm)
Wheelbase	97.8in (2,484mm)
Overall length	175.5in (4,458mm)
Overall width	71.5in (1,816mm)
Overall height	47.5in (1,207mm)
Unladen weight	
Basic kerb	2,271lb (1,030kg) (S2.2 2,469lb/1,120kg)

Performance
Top speed	125mph (201km/h) (S2.2 130mph/209km/h)
0–60mph	7.9sec (S2.2 7.8sec)

CHAPTER FOUR

THE LOTUS TYPE 89 EXCEL (1982–1992)

INTRODUCTION

The Lotus Type 89 Excel was the result of both Lotus's new relationship with the Japanese manufacturer Toyota and the ongoing development of the Elite and Eclat. While the Series 2.2 Elite and Eclat went some way towards addressing the original models' deficiencies, with galvanized chassis, Getrag gearbox and the torquier 2.2-litre engine, the Excel built on the experience of eight years of production to iron out the vast majority of the original cars' problems.

At its launch the Excel was named 'Eclat Excel' by Lotus. The Eclat part was soon dropped. GROUP LOTUS PLC

Later Excels were attractive and stylish cars. This pre-1985 car displays a strong family resemblance to the Eclat. GROUP LOTUS PLC

First introduced as the Eclat Excel in late 1982, the Excel was effectively a comprehensively reworked Eclat. By that time sales of the Elite had dropped to unsustainable levels (approximately 13 in 1981 and 14 in 1982). Sales of the Eclat were better (approximately 31 in 1981 but 162 in 1982) so the decision was taken to concentrate on the Eclat-style fastback body for the new model. The brief given to the Lotus engineers responsible for the update was to give the revised Eclat 'improved roadholding, handling, braking, and interior accommodation' and to make it 'lighter in weight, visually updated and even more competitively priced'. This was quite a strong set of requirements, but the new Eclat Excel did actually meet them.

Introduced at the Paris and British motor shows in the autumn of 1982, the Eclat Excel sported a new softer look, a completely new rear suspension package and heavily revised chassis to accommodate it, new brakes from Toyota, and an all-new, Toyota-derived drivetrain from the bell housing backwards. Retaining the Lotus 2.2 type 912 engine, the Eclat Excel also had a much revised interior and lots of subtle detail changes to the bodywork to both improve and modernize the looks and tweak the aerodynamics.

The Excel was never officially exported to the United States due to difficulties in meeting emission regulations and the ongoing problems with the pound to dollar exchange rate which made the car uncompetitive price-wise. Apparently, one car did make it to the United States, but as a right-hand drive this was likely to be a one-off.

EXCEL OPTIONS

The Excel did not use the Series 1 set of standard specifications, but had an extensive list of options that could be specified by the customer. For example, the 1988 options list included:

- Air conditioning (£1,200)
- Base half leather trim (£935)
- Base full leather (£1,780)
- SE full leather (£850)
- Metallic paint (£670)
- Pearlescent paint (£1,070)
- Eagle wheels (£320)

The Excel remained in production through to 1992, a significant length of time, and with annual sales consistently around the 200 mark the Excel was a significant and successful model for Lotus. It quickly gained a reputation for reliability and performance and was compared favourably with the mainly Japanese large-coupé competition such as the Nissan 300 ZX and the Mitsubishi/Colt Starion as well as more exotic European cars such as the Renault Alpine GTA, Jaguar XJS 3.6, Opel Monza GSE, Porsche 944, Audi Quattro and the TVR Tasmin.

LOTUS EXCEL PRODUCTION HISTORY

Entering production in 1982, the Excel was destined to have a ten-year production life. In that time it underwent numerous detail changes, gained a second model in the range – the Excel SE – in 1984, had a major facelift in 1986, and saw the introduction of an automatic version – the SA – in 1987. Sold alongside the Lotus Esprit for all its life and alongside the two-seater M100 Elan, the production of the Excel only ended in 1992 when GM pulled the plug on the company and Lotus was put into a desperate struggle for survival.

A pair of post-1985 Excels at a Lotus meet at

Brands Hatch. The red car is from 1989–90, the white car from 1985–6.

Post-1985 cars gained Audi Quattro-style flares over the front and rear wheel arches.

The Excel SE introduced at the end of 1984 had a more powerful version of the 912 2.2-litre engine with 10.0:1 compression ratio and boasting a claimed 180bhp at 6,500rpm. The car was well received by the press, and while the performance figures were not that much higher than the 'standard' model – top speed was up by 2mph and the 0–60mph time reduced by 0.2sec – the increased torque and drivability of the tuned engine made the car feel faster than the figures suggested. The SE also featured a large 'tea tray' spoiler on the boot.

At the same time as the SE was announced, the range gained a lightly revised facia with a modified heating and ventilation system; an adjustable steering column; and Audi Quattro-style blisters over the wheels, the only significant styling change to the shell. The blisters did not increase the width of the car but gave more room for wheels and tyres in the wheel arches. From then on there were minor changes to the various rear spoilers and wheels fitted, with the last visible change being a restyled bonnet with moulded-in air-extractor louvres.

Lotus was forced by its dire financial position to stop Excel production in the middle of 1992 after a successful ten-year production run with some 2,158 Excels having been produced.

The Excel SA came with the same trim levels as the SE, including the large rear spoiler.

EXCEL MECHANICALS

Engine

The Excel used the 2.2 litre 912 version of the Lotus engine throughout its production life, as described previously. The engine was initially as specified in the Series 2.2 Elite and Eclat but in 1985, when the Excel SE was launched, the engine tune was revised to give 180bhp and 150lb ft of torque.

Transmission

Lotus's tie-up with Toyota provided access to the Toyota parts bin, much to the benefit of the Eclat

Excel's all-new transmission. The clutch used Toyota components and was hydraulically operated, which was felt by the press to be a real improvement on the Elite's cable system. The car also gained a Toyota five-speed gearbox on its introduction, which was a US-market Cressida unit. The box was cheaper than the Getrag unit and performed faultlessly on the Excel. In 1988 the Excel SA was launched, which had a four-speed automatic gearbox, again sourced from Toyota. The Excel's differential was also a Toyota unit and thanks to the new rear suspension layout it no longer had to take the suspension load, so its rubber mountings could be

The Excel SE engine bay was still very similar in design to the original Elite.

lightened to simply cater for drive torque reactions and be tuned to suppress noise and vibration – thus removing in a stroke one of the Elite and Eclat's main sources of harshness. The rear drive ratio was 4.1:1 in the Excel and Excel SE, and was revised to be 3.73:1 in the Excel SA automatic version.

Chassis

The Excel chassis had a number of changes to allow fitment of the revised front and rear suspension and had a number of tweaks applied to both strengthen it and increase torsional stiffness. The most important modification however was the use of hot-dip galvanizing on the chassis. The process gave an even coating of corrosion-resistant zinc to the chassis, both on the outside and in all the box sections and nooks and crannies where water could gather. This stopped all the corrosion issues with the chassis and even today a thirty-year-old Excel chassis can be seen with its zinc coating intact

and no corrosion present. The use of a tubular rear hoop to support the rear suspension wishbone was a change from the Elite.

Suspension

The suspension used on the Excel differed in detail at the front and was radically reworked at the rear when compared with the Elite and Eclat. At the front, while it still used unequal length wishbones all components were re-engineered to make use of Toyota components. At the rear, the whole suspension set-up was redesigned to accommodate the use of Toyota components, including the differential, and to remove any suspension loadings from the driveshafts.

Front Suspension

The Excel front suspension retained the Lotus twin upper wishbones, single lower arm layout, but used

The Excel had a fully galvanized chassis. Here are a stack of second hand units at Lotusbits, all of which are fully serviceable and none showing any signs of corrosion.

The Excel's front suspension retained the original twin upper wishbones and single lower link, but used mainly Toyota components, including the ventilated disk brakes.

TONY POLL'S 1992 EXCEL

Tony Poll has owned his 1992 Excel since 2002, and is the third owner. Tony's reasons for buying the car probably sum up the Excel's current appeal – Lotus was the top Formula 1 team to many Brits in the 1970s and 1980s and Tony appreciated this and the advanced engineering they put into their road cars. Tony was attracted to a Lotus as they didn't have anything that couldn't be fixed – Tony didn't like doing rusty bodywork but normal mechanicals held no fears for him. He considered getting an Elan but thought they were a bit too basic and probably not too safe in an accident. While Tony liked the style of the Elite and Eclat, the by then well-known problems of chassis rust and potentially marginal engineering on the rear brakes, rear suspension, gearbox and lack of low down torque ruled them out. The Esprit was close, but the prospect of too many maintenance tasks in very awkward areas meant a no as well.

Tony saw that the Excel was a sufficiently fast car with great handling, a comfortable two-seat sports tourer with occasional seating for four, and was easy to maintain and had a rust-free bodyshell. With its lack of complex systems such as ABS, a normal distributor, carburettors and relatively simple mechanicals, Tony saw the Excel had lots of potential for the average owner to keep the car on the road with minimal outlay. The choice of an Excel was sealed when the sheer value for money for the car was taken into account. Tony's choice was a well-looked-

Tony Poll's 1992 Excel is one of the last ones to have been made.

Tony's Excel engine is virtually standard apart from the addition of a DTA ignition system, which operated from a crankshaft sensor and renders the distributor redundant.

after, low-mileage (40,000miles/65,000km), two-owner car which was completely standard and on which everything worked – including the air conditioning. The car drove very well, had an immaculate tan leather interior, no previous crash repairs and was in a great colour – British Racing Green. The car cost a very reasonable £10,500 – not the cheapest car on the market at the time but probably the best.

To date, Tony has not had to do much to the car. Soon after purchase the fuel pump packed up – a typical SU pump issue cured by the traditional 'SU sharp bang on the side'. Replacement electronic 'points' fitted to the fuel pump cured the problem permanently. A radiator electric fan was replaced, as was the exhausts, and the rear seat belt mounting brackets were found to be badly rusted and were replaced with stainless items from Lotusbits. The windscreen picked up a crack from a stone and was replaced, but the lower spacers weren't put in so after about five years the screen began to slide down, leaving a gap at the top.

Sometime after Tony bought the car, Lotus had a factory spares sale, so Tony took the opportunity to pick up things like calipers, springs, door seals and suspension bushes for a very reasonable price. When Tony had to go abroad for a year with his job, he packed the car off to Lotusbits to get a number of niggles sorted. They refitted the windscreen and replaced the suspension bushes, springs and dampers and steering rack, as well as carrying out a top-half respray to sort out various stone chips and marks on the sides.

Lotusbits also fitted a DTA S40 Pro mapped ignition system, which uses a crankshaft-mounted trigger sensor and a new coil pack. This replaced the distributor and made the engine much more tractable, removed a flat spot around 2,800rpm, gave more low down torque and made the car an easier starter and much nicer around town. By removing the distributor it removed the fire risk of the sparks being distributed under the carburettors.

continued overleaf

Tony Poll's 1992 Excel *continued*

Tony's Excel has a luxury interior, with leather everywhere. As the Excel production neared its end it was not uncommon for the cars to have virtually every extra specified.

Tony likes to use specialist dealers like Lotusbits and SJ Sports Cars – he has found the parts they supply do fit and likes to help to keep that sort of specialist dealer in business. Other jobs that Tony has completed included re-riveting the headlamp bobbins in place to cure the lights dancing about; replacing the front brake calipers, discs and pads; changing the door seals, as the old ones leaked; and replacing the roof lining, battery and wheel bearings. He also does his own engine maintenance, and finds it all pretty straightforward, although adjusting the valve clearance shims can be a bit messy.

Probably the fiddliest job Tony has had on his Excel was sorting out the door beams. Tony's were not badly corroded but the paint was coming off and surface rust was appearing. So

he took the doors off, cleaned the beams up and repainted them (with a bit more paint than Lotus used originally). The difficult part was getting a good fit when putting the doors back on – it was incredibly time consuming to get the fit right as it involved shimming the door with penny washers until it fitted correctly.

Compared with modern cars, Tony finds the Excel a bit crude as a GT car, but at the time it was streets ahead of the competition. He finds the performance is – to quote him – 'better than my driving' and while he usually keeps to the speed limits he has had it over the ton at one of the Club Lotus Castle Combe track days. He likes the brakes and finds them plenty powerful enough to pull the car up cleanly on the road. The DTA ignition system, as described above, makes the car

The front of Tony's Excel is distinctly Lotus in style, with the signature pop-up headlights.

more drivable and the handling has never given him any scary moments. The car is fun to drive and on its Toyo Proxy T1-R tyres has predictable handling and feels secure in fast corners.

When he bought the Excel Tony was looking for a car he can enjoy at sensible speed, and he found it in his Excel. As he says, 'It's a great car. Fast, great handling; looks great; comfortable;

gets many appreciative comments. Spare parts are readily available at reasonable cost, and there are good internet forum and community.'

Some of Tony's best moments in it have been driving over the South Downs in the early morning heading for a Goodwood classic car breakfast meet, when he can enjoy the quiet and twisty country lanes – pure Lotus country.

mainly Toyota components. The upright was supported top and bottom by swivel joints, getting rid of the Triumph threaded trunnion, and the lower arm was a forged item rather than the pressed-steel fabrication used on the Elite. The coilover shock absorber was located on the lower arm and the top passed between the two upper wishbones to locate on the chassis tower. A front anti-roll bar was located using a rubber at the outer edge of the lower arm and this assisted in the front and rear location of the arm, as in the Elite, but was a much meatier unit.

Rear Suspension

At the rear the suspension was completely revised. The Toyota-derived system maintained the Lotus geometry, but the most important change was that the driveshafts were no longer used as suspension links. No suspension forces were directed through them, so they could be lighter, and no additional forces were imposed on the differential. The suspension comprised a wide spaced asymmetric lower wishbone and a single top link. The lower wishbone front arm was

angled forwards and was located on the chassis, close to where the Elite's trailing arm was positioned, using a rubber bush and bolt. The rear arm of the lower wishbone was approximately at right angles to the chassis and was located onto a chassis frame using a detachable U-shaped rear hoop. The two top ends of the hoop were bolted to the rear cross member of the chassis just inboard of the shock absorber towers, and the centre swooped down below the level of the differential and carried a pressed steel channel. The inner ends of the rear wishbone arms were located in the outer edge of the channel on rubber bushes.

The channel was mounted onto the hoop with a single eccentric fixing that was clamped in place with a bolt, which was used to adjust the position of the channel, and hence the wishbone toe-in. The bottom of the coilover shock absorber was fixed to the rear of the outer edge of the wishbone. A light-alloy hub carrier had two lower locating lugs which were bolted onto the edge of the wishbone using rubber bushes to allow the hub carrier to move perpendicular to the wishbone. A single tubular upper link arm bolted to the top of the carrier, with the inner end mounted on the chassis to make

The Excel's rear suspension differed radically from the Elites. With upper and lower links the drive shafts do not have any suspension loads, and the outboard disk brakes were a major improvement on the elite's inboard drums.

the rear suspension completely independent of the driveshafts – both ends of the link arm were rubber bushed. The driveshafts connected to a short outboard driveshaft carried in the hub carrier and was supported on a pair of roller bearings. Each driveshaft had a constant velocity joint at each end to allow for suspension movement.

Brakes and Steering
Toyota strikes again – the front discs and calipers were both Toyota items and at the rear there were outboard discs, again with Toyota calipers. At the front, the 10.16in-diameter ventilated discs were gripped by single-piston sliding calipers which performed well and marked a move away from the solid discs fitted to the Elite. At the rear there was a major improvement with the replacement of the inboard drums with outboard discs. Like the front, the rear discs were also ventilated but they were 10.5in-diameter units (surprisingly larger than the front units), and were again gripped by slightly smaller Toyota single-piston sliding calipers mounted on the new cast-alloy rear hub carrier.

The handbrake was also redesigned, comprising a pair of small drums bolted onto the rear of the discs and cable operated from the lever on the centre tunnel.

Steering was by rack-and-pinion, with power assistance as an option. At the time, the power steering was praised for giving more feel than the rather light system fitted to the Elite and Eclat.

Body
The Excel body was broadly similar to the Eclat Series 2.2 unit but had a large number of minor changes. The body still consisted of a pair of top and bottom mouldings with built-in reinforcement made by the VARI process, and glued together. Changes included a new nose, bumpers, bonnet, window line, sills, boot and under tray. Sill trims complemented the extended front spoiler, which was similar to the S2 item, and the rear bumper was modified from the Series 2.2 to allow a full-width, UK-specification number plate to be fitted between the Rover SD1 rear lights. The bright window surrounds of the Series 2.2 models were replaced with thinner, satin-black fittings and the rear C-pillar was covered in a body-coloured moulding, which tidied up the rear quarter of the car.

Throughout its life the Excel had various graphics applied. This pre-1985 car features the original non-flared wheel arches. GROUP LOTUS PLC

This 1987 car displays the Excel's post-1985 modified body with flared wheel arches.

From the front it is hard to believe that the Excel is a roomy 2+2 coupé.

Late Excel interiors are nice places to be. This is Martin Bradley's 1991 Excel SE.

The introduction of the SE in October 1985 saw a small rubber bib added to the bottom of the front spoiler and the SE acquired a new larger rear spoiler. Some minor styling changes were made throughout the Excel's life, the first coming in 1986 with the introduction of subtle flares to the front and rear wheel arches in order to accommodate larger wheels, although there was no increase in the overall width of the body.

Interior and Electrics

Interior
On its introduction, the Excel's interior was broadly similar to the Series 2.2 cars with a similar dash layout incorporating the more modern switches and warning lights. Ground glass covered the minor dials in order to cut down reflections and the whole cabin was nicely trimmed. As the car aged, the interior was upgraded at regular intervals and leather upholstery became more common. As the Excel was a low-production car, many of the cars would have been produced to order, with their interior trim specified from the options list.

Around October 1985 and the introduction of the SE, Lotus ditched the Smiths gauges used since the introduction of the Elite and switched to Italian supplier VDO to supply its instruments.

Electrics
The Excel inherited the Elite and Excel's 12-volt negative earth electrics. The system remained basically unchanged until the cars gained central locking and an ice warning system as standard in late 1987.

Specials
The Excel Celebration was produced in 1991 to commemorate Lotus's twenty-fifth year in the Hethel plant. There were a total of 40 cars produced, 35 in Celebration Green Metallic and 5 in Calypso Red. The main specification change was a full-leather interior in tan, including the steering wheel, and Wilton wool carpets throughout. A top specification Clarion stereo was mated with a six-CD stacker in the boot. These cars were produced alongside the last Excels made as production numbers were declining through 1991-92 as the car reached the end of its life.

LOTUS EXCEL (1982–92) SPECIFICATIONS

Layout and chassis   Two door, 2+2 seat sports coupé with glass-reinforced plastic body, conventional rear boot and separate steel chassis and rear-wheel drive.

Engine

Type	Lotus 45-degree slant-4
Block material	Die-cast light alloy
Head material	Die cast light alloy
Cylinders	4 in line
Cooling	Water/antifreeze mix
Bore and stroke	95.29 x 76.2mm
Capacity	2172cc
Valves	4 valves per cylinder, operated by belt-driven dohc
Compression ratio	9.4:1 (SE, SA 10.9:1)
Carburettor	Twin Dellorto twin choke DHLA 45E (SE, SA DHLA 45D)
Max. power (claimed)	160bhp at 6,500rpm (SE, SA180bhp at 6,500rpm)
Max. torque	160lb ft at 5,000rpm (SE, SA 165lb ft at 5,000rpm)
Fuel capacity	14.8gal (67ltr)

Transmission

Gearbox (manual)		Toyota five-speed all synchromesh
Clutch		Single dry plate
Ratios	1st	3.29:1
	2nd	1.89:1
	3rd	1.27:1
	4th	1.00:1
	5th	0.78:1
	Reverse	3.769:1
Gearbox (SA auto)		ZF four-speed automatic
Ratios	1st	2.73:1
	2nd	1.56:1
	3rd	1.0:1
	4th	0.73:1
	Reverse	2.09:1
Final drive		4.1:1 (SA auto 3.73:1)

Suspension and Steering

Front	Independent by upper twin wishbones, single lower link, anti-roll bar, coil springs over telescopic dampers
Rear	Independent by lower wishbone, upper transverse link, coil springs over telescopic dampers
Steering	Rack-and-pinion (power operated option)
Tyres	205/60 VR 14 radial (SE 215/50 VR 15 radial)
Wheels	Alloy 14in (SE 7JK x 15in-diameter cast aluminium alloy
Rim width	7in

Brakes

Type	Front and rear discs with servo assistance
Size	10.16in front, 10.5in rear

Dimensions

Track		
	Front	57.5in (1,460mm)
	Rear	57.5in (1,460mm)
Wheelbase		97.8in (2,484mm)
Overall length		172.3in (4,376mm)
Overall width		71.5in (1,816mm)
Overall height		47.5in (1,207mm)
Unladen weight		
	Basic kerb	2,486lb (1,128kg)

Performance

Top speed		130mph (209km/h)
	SE	132mph (212km/h)
	SA	129mph (208km/h)
0–60mph		7.1sec
	SE	6.9sec
	SA	8.8sec

CHAPTER FIVE

OWNING AND RUNNING

The Elite, Eclat and Excel have for many years been the poor relations of the Lotus family. Not as sporty or attractive as the 1960s' Elan and Plus 2, with definitive 1970s 'wedge' styling and low residual values, the family has languished in the classic car doldrums through the 1990s and the noughties. Those in the know have long recognized that the combination of superb roadholding and handling, rust-free body, strong engine, good performance and a virtually unique style makes for a practical and economical to run classic car.

At the time of writing, the cars were the cheapest way into Lotus ownership, and while the Elite's styling is not to everybody's taste, the couple style of the Eclat and Excel are attractive and sporty with more than enough room for a couple of passengers in the back. At last the cars are beginning to enjoy a revival – their value for money is being appreciated, their styling is now becoming fashionable once more and their undoubted practicality make them a viable classic for a family – if you take one to a show the kids can come too!

Rust

One of the major plus points of running an Elite, Eclat or Excel is their use of rust-free glass fibre for the body. However, the cars are not immune from the dreaded tin worm as there are several components, including the chassis, which were made from steel sheet. The early Elite and Eclat chassis had

The Elite, Eclat and Excel were all produced in Lotus's Hethel factory in Norfolk, UK. GROUP LOTUS PLC

The extra bulge on the Eclat's bonnet hides a Rover V8 – there is plenty of room to fit the Rover unit.

only minimal rustproofing in the form of a thin coat of paint and so do rust; the most likely area being the cross member above the differential which is difficult to see when the body is on the chassis. In addition, the rear seat belt mounting plate, to which the top mounts of the rear seat belts bolt, are also prone to rust, rendering the rear belts prone to pulling off the mount when they are most needed. Rust can also attack the door beams, weakening them to the extent that the door's structural integrity can be lost and the side-impact protection given by the beams being greatly reduced. However, none of these issues, with the exception of the chassis, are terminal, and can be relatively easy to repair. For true longevity a galvanized chassis, as fitted to the Series 2.2 Elite and Eclat and the Excel, is perfect – and although it is a big job, it is perfectly possible for a competent home mechanic to do a chassis swap.

Bodywork

The body on all the cars is robust and thanks to the VARI system is a lot less prone to stress cracking than the earlier Lotuses – especially the original Elans. As the body has gel coat on both sides it is also properly sealed and has a good finish which is easy to keep clean on areas such as the engine bay and under the carpets. There is nothing special about the body and standard glass-fibre repair techniques (described in the workshop manual) work well and are easily done by a competent home mechanic.

Mechanicals

Mechanically the cars are better the later the model. The main potentially dangerous fault that has emerged over the years is the rear suspension pivot bolts on the Elite and Eclat. These are prone to breaking; Lotus changed the specification of the material used to make the bolts during the lifetime of the car to specify ever-stronger steel. Genuine replacements are not cheap but should always be used as the consequences of a failed bolt are serious. The rest of the mechanicals are pretty good.

Engine

The cam covers on the 907 engine are prone to leaking but Lotusbits can supply better gaskets; otherwise there are no inherent faults with the engines. The specialists recommend that the originally recommended Valvoline 20/50 multigrade mineral oil is used. The cars shouldn't overheat as long as the cooling ducting has not been disturbed and the cooling fan or fans are working – if original fans are fitted, make sure they do still work correctly as underuse or old age makes them prone to seize. As the engine is all alloy, the recommended antifreeze mixture should be used to protect against frost damage and corrosion. The cam belt must be changed at the recommended intervals and it is worth changing the tensioner wheel and bearing at the same time.

Transmission

The five-speed Lotus gearbox is not strong, and most still in use will probably have been rebuilt by now, but look out for noise and lack of synchromesh as these are signs of impending doom. The boxes can be rebuilt, but replacement with a Getrag box is probably a better bet. The Borg Warner automatic boxes fitted to the Elites and Eclats are good, reliable units but can often benefit from a transmission fluid change. The Toyota gearboxes (manual and automatic) on the Excel appear to go on forever!

Suspension

The suspension on the Elite and Eclat is relatively simple and easy for the home mechanic to maintain; swivel joints, the lower trunnion and wheel bearings all can wear at the front, while at the rear the wheel bearings (another Austin Maxi part) wears.

The Elite's side profile shows the slightly heavy looking rear quarter needed to accommodate four full-sized passengers.

This Series 1 Elite is parked in front of the car it replaced in the Lotus range, the Elan Plus 2.

Most of the bushes in the suspension are rubber and seem to last pretty well but original cars can start to feel quite loose when the rubber starts to perish.

The main issue with the suspension is corrosion of the various bolts – the front trunnion through bolts are notorious for seizing onto their steel spacing tubes. It can be a tricky job to get them out without damaging the lower suspension arm.

Driveshaft universal joints can fail and it is imperative that good-quality replacements are used. A cheap unit from eBay is virtually guaranteed to break quickly as it will not be able to handle the relatively high loads imposed on it as result of the driveshaft taking the suspension loads. The Excel's suspension is relatively trouble free, with the fabled Toyota reliability and quality engineering meaning

that failures and faults, other than general wear, are rare.

At the rear, bolts can seize in the alloy hub carrier – usually they can be freed off with the judicious application of heat.

Brakes

The front brakes are conventional although the discs are not cheap to replace, but the rear drums are inaccessible, prone to oil contamination from the differential and are generally a pain to work on.

Interior

Finally interior trim for all the cars is getting hard to find and a tatty interior can cost a fortune to get back into a reasonable state.

MARTIN BRADLEY'S 1991 LOTUS EXCEL SE

Martin Bradley is a bit of a Lotus fan – he has owned three Lotus Sunbeams, two Excels and one Esprit, and was introduced to the delights of Lotus driving by his father who took him on a test drive in an Elan Sprint at the tender and impressionable age of eleven or twelve. Since then he has owned a succession of 900-powered Lotus models, and currently owns a bright red 1991 Excel SE which he bought in 2013 for a reasonable £3,750.

Since he has had the Excel Martin has had virtually no problems with it. He replaced all four tyres – the ones that came with the car were old and perished – and has had to rebuild one brake caliper which had seized. Suitable tyres were quite hard to find; they were 215/50 x 15 and the only ones he could find were made by Dunlop but he is happy with them. In his experience the Toyota mechanicals used on the Excel are pretty much bulletproof – his previous two Excels also gave him few problems. For engine oil he always uses the recommended Valvoline 20/50, and the only thing wrong with his Excel at the moment is the headlining – it had dropped down so Martin has taken it out and is looking for a local trimmer to refit it at a reasonable price. He also feels that the brakes could be improved – new Aeroquip flexible brake pipes are on the shopping list.

With its bright red exterior the Excel is a lovely car to look at and to be seen in – one high spot of

continued overleaf

**The final Excels were handsome cars and give practical and reliable motoring.
This is Martin Bradley's example in gleaming red.**

Martin Bradley's 1991 Excel interior shows how luxurious the Excel is for the driver and passengers.

Even with the headlamps up the clean lines of Martin's Excel are not compromised.

Martin Bradley's 1991 Lotus Excel SE *continued*

his ownership was when Martin was asked about his 'Ferrari' while he was in his local high street; he thinks the colour may have confused the questioner but also thinks the shape and style of the Lotus are superb in their own right.

With an all-leather interior and wood trim Martin's car is a nice place for the driver (and passengers) to be in, and the relatively modern cockpit gives off a definite feeling of quality mixed in with a promise of performance. While the theoretical top speed is somewhere around 130mph (209km/h), Martin finds the car will comfortably and effortlessly get up to an indicated 90mph (145km/h) on the German Autobahns and is reasonably quiet and refined. Roadholding is superb (especially with the new rubber) while handling is typical Lotus – it goes round corners 'like it is on rails' and the ride is not harsh or intrusive at all – in fact it is quite soft and comfortable.

Martin has always loved the way Lotuses both look and drive, and thinks his Excel is an excellent sports coupé that has managed to achieve a difficult brief – to maintain the Lotus DNA in a family-friendly package.

RIGHT: **Martin Bradley's son Christopher enjoys riding in the Excel with his dad.**

BELOW: **Long and low, the Excel's sleek profile still bears some styling cues from the Elite. As a package, the Excel is hard to beat if you want a roomy 2+2 coupé with a racing heritage.**

What to Buy?

If you want a true example of Chapman and Lotus's design, faults and all, then a Series 1 Elite or Eclat is the truest incarnation of the design brief. With its terrifically 1970s cabin styling and materials (as well as the built-in mechanical issues), it accurately reflects the state of the art in the mid-1970s. In the author's opinion the Elite also probably just pips the Eclat to the post due to its more radical styling, but that is a purely personal opinion and the Eclat's coupé looks are preferred by many.

A Series 2.2 car offers a lot more, including a less mad interior, enhanced reliability with its Getrag gearbox and galvanized chassis, and more accessible performance – again the Elite and Eclat are only separated by their styling.

The Excel is actually a superb car, with a luxury feel with a great performance along with massively improved reliability. The only downside to the Excel is that it is only available in coupé form. However, it is always possible to put an Elite body onto an Excel chassis, a practice that is becoming more common and allowing owners to have the classic Elite looks and practicality with the Excel's reliability and drivability.

RESOURCES FOR THE ELITE, ECLAT AND EXCEL OWNER

There are a vast range of resources open to the Elite, Eclat and Excel owner and enthusiast. These range from the printed word in books and magazines to clubs, helpful and friendly dealers, and finally the internet. The following sections give the current state of the Lotus Elite, Eclat and Excel world.

The Elite is a restrained and classy design, and is really unlike any other car.

At the time of writing (2015), the Lotus archivist is Andy Graham who looks after the build records for all production-built Lotus road cars. The current contact details of the Lotus archivist can be obtained from Lotus direct (see www.lotuscars.com) or through the various Lotus clubs or the www.Lotus-Elan.net and www.LotusExcel.net websites. Lotus is able to help with production dates, original supplying dealers and build details of the Lotus Elite, Eclat and Excel, as well as heritage certificates for the original specification of a specific car. The original factory workshop manuals and parts-listing books are also available from Lotus dealers.

Books

If a reader is contemplating buying and restoring an Elite, Eclat or Excel model there are a pair of publications that are essential: the official Lotus Workshop Manual and the Service Parts List. These are available new from most Lotus specialists, and second-hand copies come up on eBay and Amazon frequently. There are two distinct pairs of documents – one for the Elite and Eclat and a second for the Excel. The workshop manual gives technical details of the cars and instructions on dismantling and reassembling them, while the Service Parts List gives exploded diagrams of all the cars' sub-assemblies and the parts numbers of every part used in the car; the diagrams in the Service Parts List also show the order of assembly of each sub-assembly.

The following books were used by the author in the writing of this book, and provide additional information and details on the Elite, Eclat and Excel and other aspects of the Lotus story. While some of the books are out of print, second-hand copies are usually available through online sources such as Amazon or eBay.

Adcock, Ian, *Lotus Heritage* (Osprey, year, ISBN 1-85532-508-X) A well-illustrated book that traces Lotus road cars' developments from the original Elite to the M100 Elan, covering the Elite, Eclat and Excel family.

Arnold, Graham, *Illustrated Lotus Buying Guide* (Motorbooks International, year, ISBN 0-87938-217-1) Written by the former Lotus marketing director, this book covers buying Lotus road cars ranging from the VI and Seven through to the Esprit, and has a reasonable section on the original Elite and Eclat.

Clarke, R. M., *Lotus Elite and Eclat, 1974 – 1982, A Brooklands Road Test Portfolio* (Brooklands Books, year, ISBN 978-1-85520-917-6) A compilation of road tests and articles on the Elite and Eclat which cover from the car's launch in 1974 through to articles from classic car magazines in the 2000s. Not to be missed, a very good value for money book with loads of contemporary information inside.

Clarke, R. M., *Lotus Excel, A Brooklands Road Test Portfolio* (Brooklands Books, year, ISBN 978-1-85520-918-3) A compilation of launch reports, road tests and articles on the Excel from 1982 through to 2002. Like all Brooklands road test volumes a very good value for money book with loads of contemporary information.

Crombac, Gerard 'Jabby', *Colin Chapman – The Man and His Cars* (Haynes Publishing Group, year, ISBN 1-85960-844-2) This is the authorized biography of Chapman, written by a long term Lotus owner and fan who was also a noted Formula 1 journalist. It gives a comprehensive picture of the man and the evolution of his company up to Chapman's death in 1982.

Harvey, Chris, *Lotus – The Complete Story* (Haynes Publishing Group, year, ISBN 0-85429-298-5) A history of Lotus from its inception to the early 1980s. While primarily a company history it includes some details on the Elite.

Hayes, Russell, *Lotus – The Creative Edge* (Haynes Classic Makes Series, year, ISBN 978-1-84425-249-7. This is a general history of Lotus up to 2007 which focuses on the road cars and has a chapter on the Elite and Eclat.

Lawrence, Mike, *Colin Chapman Wayward Genius* (Brooklands Books, year, ISBN 978-1-85520-950-3) Originally published by Breedon Books (ISBN 1-85983-278-4), this biography of Chapman covers his achievements in a 'warts and all' fashion and makes for an interesting read, giving alternative interpretation of many of the legends that have grown around Chapman.

Ludigsen, Karl, *Colin Chapman – Inside the Innovator* (Haynes Publishing Group, year, ISBN 978-1-84425-413-2) A comprehensive account of

The Elite's rear was pretty much unique styling-wise at the time, with a low and wide stance and large rear hatch.

Colin Chapman's engineering achievements, based around themed chapters looking at specific topics, such as suspension, downforce, structures etc.

Robson, Graham, *Lotus Since the 70s – Volume 1: Elite, Eclat, Excel and Elan* (Motor Racing Publications Ltd, year, ISBN 0-94798-170-5) This volume superseded Robson's 1983 book The Third Generation Lotuses and covers the complete history of the Elite, Eclat and Excel in some detail.

Wilkins, Miles, *Fibreglass Bodywork* (Osprey Publishing, year, ISBN0-85045-556-1) Miles Wilkins of Fibreglass Services provides the inside knowledge of glass fibre repair and restoration, essential for any Lotus restorer.

Dealers

The author has a 1969 Elan Plus 2S which he is currently restoring from a pile of bits and has owned a later Lotus Elite. The following dealers in the UK have either been responsible for supplying parts for the Elite or been recommended to the author by other Lotus owners and as such can be recommended:

Lotusbits Ltd, Unit F, Old Station Yard, Oxford Road, Marton, Warwickshire, CV23 9RU, Tel: 01926 633 211, www.lotusbits.com. Specializes in the Elite, Eclat and Excel. Supplies new and second-hand parts and complete cars and carries out servicing, mechanical work and can do complete restorations.

Paul Matty Sports Cars Ltd, 12 Old Birmingham Road, Bromsgrove, Worcestershire, B60 1DE, Tel: +44 (0)1527 835 656, Email: enquiries@paulmatty-sportscars.co.uk, www.paulmattysportscars.co.uk. Parts and cars.

Christopher Neil (part of Oakmere Motor Group), Christopher Neil Limited, Manchester Road, Northwich, Cheshire, CW9 7NA, Tel: +44 (0)844

Lotuses always look good in yellow and the Elite is no exception.

662 7224, www.oakmeremotorgroup.co.uk/lotus. Parts and cars.

SJ Sportscars Limited, Unit 1 Ash Down End, Lords Meadow Industrial Estate, Crediton, Devon, EX17 1HN, Tel: +44 (0)1363 777 790, Email: steve@sjs-portscars.co.uk, www.sjsportscars.co.uk. Stocks lots of spares for the Elite, Eclat and Excel.

QED Motor Sport Ltd, 4 Soar Road, Quorn, Leicestershire, LE12 8BN, Tel: +44 (0)1509 412 317, http://qedmotorsport.co.uk/. A good source of quality parts for the Lotus 900 series engine.

Clubs
Club Lotus is (to quote the club) 'the worlds first and biggest club for all Lotus enthusiasts'. It supports many local areas, and has a good-quality quarterly magazine and organizes and runs national and local events throughout the year. It has recently set up the Club Lotus Elan Section, providing a rich source of Elan-specific information, hints and tips for the members. Contact details: Club Lotus, 58 Malthouse Court, Dereham, Norfolk, NR20 4UA, Tel +44(0)1362 694 459/691 144, Email (membership enquiries): annemarie@clublotus.co.uk, www.clublotus.co.uk.

Lotus Drivers Club was set up in 1976 in the West Midlands and has now grown to have branches across the UK. It supports many UK events and has a magazine, Chicane, which is published every four months. Contact details: Lotus Drivers Club, PO Box 9292, Alcester, Warwickshire, B50 4LD, Email: admin@lotusdriversclub.org.uk, www.lotus-driverclub.org.uk.

The last Excels were classy and classic cars.

Internet

There are a myriad of Lotus-related sites on the internet. The following are those that the author has found useful while writing this book and working on his Elite:

The Lotus Forums at www.thelotusforums.com cover all the Lotus ranges and has a dedicated forum for the Elite, Eclat and Excel.

The Lotus Excel-specific site www.lotusexcel.net website covers the Excel in detail, with forums, and also has threads for the earlier cars. Well worth a visit.

The Lotus Drivers Guide website has been created to collect information on all Lotus cars including the Elite, Eclat and Excel. It is a useful source of information on the cars, books, brochures, history etc. http://www.lotusdriversguide.com/index.htm

The Golden Gate Lotus Club website has a huge amount of Lotus-related information, with lots on Elite and Eclat. It also gives details of this US-based Lotus club's activities. http://www.gglotus.org/

The existing Lotus Company is aware of its heritage and can be found at www.lotuscars.com.

The only other resource that I would like to mention is eBay – this worldwide auction site has revolutionized the buying and selling of all sorts of things, including Lotus Elites, Eclats and Excels. From the smallest part to complete running cars, the author has used eBay to buy many hard to find parts at reasonable prices. It's a bit like having every local paper's classified adverts ready to hand to buy and sell.

MIKE TAYLOR AND LOTUSBITS

Mike Taylor runs Lotusbits Ltd, located at Unit F, Old Station Yard, Oxford Road, Marton, Warwickshire, CV23 9RU. Mike's interest in the four-seater Lotus family started in 1992 when he bought an Elite which he started to restore, but found parts were both expensive and elusive. In the mid-1990s he ended up buying a 'spares' car for £350 to assist in keeping his Elite on the road. Other Elite owners heard about it and Mike started to buy complete cars to break and supply second-hand spares to Elite and Eclat owners as a hobby. With his hobby taking up more and more of his time, in 2005 Mike bought a local industrial estate to house the operation and converted his hobby into a full-time occupation. Today Mike presides over what must be the only business dedicated to the Elite, Eclat and Excel and can provide a bewildering range of new or used parts for the cars, as well as mechanical services ranging from a simple service to a full restoration.

Lotusbits as a business has four main areas:

• Second-hand parts taken from cars which have been broken specifically for parts

• Remanufactured parts – if there is enough demand Lotusbits will commission the remanufacture or refurbishment of parts
• Workshop Services – routine servicing, rebuilding and restoring
• Performance upgrades and competition preparation

With an extensive store of new and used parts, Mike can supply virtually anything for the 907/912-engined Lotuses including the Esprit. Mike has for some time been getting hard to find parts remanufactured, often improving them as well when needed. The type of things Mike is making available to the spares market include replated suspension bolts (originals are no longer available), remanufactured cam belt auto-tensioner plungers, piston rings, pistons and connecting rods. The race-proved Lotusbits pistons and connecting rods are significantly lighter but still stronger than the standard items. He can supply reworked performance cylinder heads, which are gas flowed and have larger

continued overleaf

Mike Taylor own Lotusbits, and has worked with the Elite Eclat and Excel family of Lotuses (and the Esprit) for many years.

Mike Taylor and LotusBits *continued*

valves, and have remanufactured gaskets, oil seals, power-steering pipes, alloy header tanks, clutch plates, lightweight flywheels, radiators and even graphics and decals. On top of this Mike can also supply second-hand parts from the cars he breaks, ranging from a minor item of trim to a complete engine. One of Mike's specialist services is re-engineering Elites and Eclats with the Excel chassis and running gear to give all the advantages of the Excel to Elite owners – basically mixing the best of both models.

With his long-term experience of running, restoring, working on and breaking Elites, Eclats and Excels, Mike is well placed to identify what is good and what is bad about the cars. He maintains that all the cars in the Elite family have a fantastic engine and wonderful handling. The no-rust fibreglass body is a major plus and the cars, when in good condition, are incredibly safe – the award of the Don Trophy proved this at the time and even today the cars show up well against modern vehicles. On the downside, the Lotus five-speed gearbox is, in Mike's own words, 'a chocolate fireguard' and really rather fragile. The Series 1 cars' chassis was not galvanized and it rots – the paint fell off and some cars had their chassis replaced when they were only two to three years old. The differential seals are prone to leak, contaminating the rear brake shoes and drums and the universal joints in the driveshafts are weak. Mike recommends the best-quality ones be used, but even these have a limited life. The Austin Maxi rear wheel bearings are weak, and can only be made to last with expensive grease, and all in all Mike describes the early rear suspension set-up as evil. The front suspension uses Triumph Herald brass trunnions which seize if not regularly oiled, and the rear seat-belt mounts are made of mild steel and will rust away – Lotusbits supplies them remanufactured in stainless steel. The door beams were, like the chassis, poorly painted from the factory, and as the interior of the door is wet they rot – and in the worst case the door falls off!

For the Series 2.2 Lotus used electric operation for the pop-up headlamps which while better than the original vacuum system used unreliable Lucas motors (as seen on the Triumph TR7) to power them but at least the car didn't end up 'winking' to all and sundry while parked and the vacuum leaked out. The five-speed Getrag gearbox was solid and reliable, and a galvanized chassis cured the corrosion problem at a stroke. The Excel cured most other things – with Toyota suspension

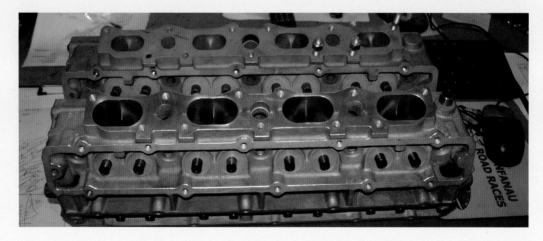

Lotusbits have lots of experience in improving the cars – here is a reworked cylinder head ready to give an Excel a performance boost.

front and rear, although the Lotus front wishbone arms and uprights were carried over, the Toyota ball joints, brakes, manual gearbox and differential were (and are) all bulletproof. The revised rear suspension, where there is no suspension force on the driveshafts and differential, also removed all the rear suspension woes of the earlier cars. And of course Lotusbits can convert an Elite or Eclat to use the Excel chassis and suspension for the best of both worlds.

Mike also branched out into Sunbeam Lotus cars, running a pair of rally-prepared cars. He had a bit of a twist to the original Sunbeam as he basically cuts out the bottom of the original Sunbeam body and welds in an Excel chassis and running gear. As Mike says, it 'actually makes them handle properly'. As well as the rally preparation, Mike also supplies a range of new, reconditioned and remanufactured parts for these largely forgotten rally champions.

Lotusbits is a well-established concern with a deep knowledge of the Lotus four-seater family. The knowledge is based on solid experience and engineering skills and, in the author's experience, any owner of one of the cars can be assured of great service from Mike's team.

Lotusbits also remanufactures or refurbishes parts. Here are a batch of new rubber parts, new piston rings and refurbished and replated suspension bolts.

Mike Taylor of Lotusbits also runs a couple of Lotus Talbot Sunbeams with reworked 900 series engines. The mechanicals all sit on cut-and-shut Excel chassis to make the cars handle better.

A last look at the car that started it all – the Elite.

INDEX

Acryonitrile Butadiene Styrene (ABS) 71, 73, 74, 83
Artioli, Romano 22
Aston Martin 10, 84, 85
Audi 77, 110, 112
Austin Seven 14
Austin Maxi 7, 56, 128, 140
Autocar magazine 50

Bedford 46
Borg Warner 26, 29, 54, 57, 94, 97, 106, 128
Bradley, Martin 123, 130
Bristol 87
British Standards 83
Bugatti 22
Burr, Ron 42
Burman 64

Castle Combe 38, 39, 105, 118
Chapman, Colin 14, 15, 16, 17, 18, 21, 22, 23, 24,
    25, 30, 31, 33, 36, 37, 38, 42, 46, 53, 60, 65,
    68, 70, 71, 78, 86, 87, 134, 135, 136
Club Lotus 38, 105, 118, 137
Coventry Climax 19, 42, 86, 87
Chrysler 50
Coefficient of Drag (CD) 77, 78, 99

Dellorto 53, 55, 94, 106, 124
Don Safety Trophy 8, 15, 25, 71
Dunlop 64, 130

Earls Court Motor show 19, 26

Federal (cars) 46, 48, 53, 104

General Motors (GM) 18, 22, 42,110
Getrag 27, 30, 51, 56, 57, 58, 88, 92, 94, 106, 108,
    113, 128, 134, 140
Giugiaro, Giorgetto 78

GKN 64, 65
Glaverbel 73
Golden Gate Lotus 138,
Goodyear 64, 105
Greenham, Leigh 27, 30
GRP – Glass Reinforced plastic 8, 86

Hethel 17, 18, 21, 24, 38, 52, 123, 126

Italdesign 78

Jensen Healey 46, 49, 50, 51, 53

Kimberley, Mike 15, 16, 22, 24

Lotus Drivers Club 137
Lotus (the company) 14–22, 128
Lotus Models:
    Elan 6, 12, 15, 19, 21, 22, 23, 25, 53, 56, 58, 59,
        60, 64, 65, 68, 70, 73, 80, 87, 101, 116, 126,
        127, 130, 136, 137
    Elan M100 110
    Elite (Model 14) 19, 23, 58, 87
    Esprit 15, 21, 22, 27, 29, 31, 38, 46, 102, 110,
        116, 130, 135, 139
    Etna 46
    Europa 15, 21, 25, 42, 46,
    Plus 2 6, 12, 13, 15, 21, 23, 24, 42, 56, 58, 60,
        64, 71, 73, 81, 96, 126, 129, 136
    6 (VI) 14, 19
Lotus Engines:
    Twin Cam 20, 21, 41, 53,
    Type 904/905/906 46
    Type 907 7, 23, 25, 42, 46, 49, 51, 53, 54, 88,
        128, 139
    Type 908/909 46
    Type 912 53, 54, 88, 109, 112, 113, 139
    Type LV220 46

Le Mans 15, 19, 41, 86
Lotusbits 115, 117, 118, 128, 136, 139
Lucas 83, 140
Lumenition 31, 48, 54

Maximar 87
MG 13, 57
MIRA 77, 78

Philips radio 83
Poll, Tony 116
Production figures and dates 11, 12, 28

Saab 42
Salisbury differential 58
Sanville, Steve 42
Sheet Moulding Compound (SMC) 64, 65
Society of Motor Manufacturers and Traders
    (SMMT) 23
Speedline 32, 66
Stromberg 46, 53, 94, 104, 106
SU 87

Taylor, Mike 139
Toyota 10, 18, 22, 29, 56, 58, 102, 108, 109, 113,
    114, 120, 121, 124, 128, 129, 130, 141
Triumph Models:
    Dolomite 42, 57
    GT6 60, 64
    Herald 60, 140
    Spitfire 60

Urethane foam 69, 70

Vandevell 48
VARI process 68, 70, 121, 127
Vauxhall 42, 46, 50,

Walsh, John 105
Winterbottom, Oliver 15, 16, 24
VW-Audi Group 77